PERSIST
HOW TO BEAT THE THINGS THAT MAKE US QUIT.

CLARENCE M. LEE, JR. MD, MBA

authorHOUSE

AuthorHouse™
1663 Liberty Drive
Bloomington, IN 47403
www.authorhouse.com
Phone: 1 (800) 839-8640

© 2017 CLARENCE M. LEE, JR. MD, MBA. All rights reserved.

No part of this book may be reproduced, stored in a retrieval system, or transmitted by any means without the written permission of the author.

Published by AuthorHouse 07/06/2017

ISBN: 978-1-5246-9556-9 (sc)
ISBN: 978-1-5246-9554-5 (hc)
ISBN: 978-1-5246-9555-2 (e)

Library of Congress Control Number: 2017908792

Print information available on the last page.

Any people depicted in stock imagery provided by Thinkstock are models, and such images are being used for illustrative purposes only.
Certain stock imagery © Thinkstock.

This book is printed on acid-free paper.

Because of the dynamic nature of the Internet, any web addresses or links contained in this book may have changed since publication and may no longer be valid. The views expressed in this work are solely those of the author and do not necessarily reflect the views of the publisher, and the publisher hereby disclaims any responsibility for them.

"Clarence Lee is an overcomer. But he is more than that. He is a teacher and trainer in life skills that can help you overcome as well. Read *Persist* and learn not only how to prevail over adversity, but how to equip yourself with passion and purpose that will fuel your journey for today and all your tomorrows."
—John Jackson, PhD, president, William Jessup University

Dr. John Jackson is the author of books on leadership, cultural transformation, and spiritual formation.

"You can live life or you can live life on your path with a unique purpose that not only fulfills your own personal desires but those around you. I love Clarence's work when it comes to getting on your path and living your dreams. When you're finished reading this book, there won't be an excuse left. You either want to live life on your path or exist amongst the billions of others wondering what life would have been like if they just took action."
—Tony Hoffman, former BMX elite pro; founder, Freewheel Project; APB substance-abuse speaker

"In *Persist*, Dr. Lee develops an infrastructure for success, through detailing the barriers to goal achievement and deconstructing the ways to overcome them. His system is universally valuable, from the boardroom to the weight room."
—Torence Powell, dean of communication, visual and performing arts, Cosumnes River College

"This is both powerful and provocative! You have managed to take some commonsense notions and expand on them in more contemporary contextual themes that can be applied to everyday situations. The chapter on 'Fear' demonstrates the internal triggers and mental mechanisms we adopt to self-sabotage ourselves. This should be required reading for the age groups you identified. For African American men, it is a powerful antidote."
—Dr. Eric V. Gravenberg, president/CEO, The Hawk Institute

"*Persist* is a *must-read* book for everyone! Dr. Clarence Lee shows you how to persist and overcome the obstacles and excuses that everyone has along the path to reaching their goals. He discusses the most common excuses that people have and very specific solutions to them. After reading this book, I am even more inspired to reach my goals, and I'm positive you will be inspired and motivated as well."
—Antonio J. Webb, MD, orthopedic resident surgeon, motivational speaker, and author of *Overcoming the Odds*. More information can be found at www.antoniowebbmd.com.

"We can *all* agree that fear has its way with us when we don't take action against it. I like the 'can-do' prescription Dr. Lee has outlined in his book *Persist* to help us overcome and walk past fear. As a former NFL player, I realized that it is better to be hyper-focused on taking action than it is to fear the risks. He unfolds the process psychologically and scientifically and puts it into layman's terms for the reader. Dr. Lee is an inspiration to so many people by not only writing but he walks the walk. Everyone should have this book readily available on your nightstand or in your office. It's *empowering*!
—Michael Harper, former NFL running back, athletic director, William Jessup University

"*Persist* wonderfully demonstrates what business and social-science research have validated. It is the attitude brought to the struggle that determines if you win or lose—are successful or not. This book should be read by every young person—especially those who feel the world is against them, those who believe they are not smart enough, and those who contemplate just giving up.

"*Persist* is more proof, as Angela Duckworth's book *Grit* (firmness of character, indomitable spirit, perseverance, and passion) points out is the key to success. The ability to persist is framed by the attitude of individuals. This book will help those who read it understand earlier than most that it is their attitude and their indomitable spirit that will determine if they reach their life goals. Whether they are successful or not is not determined by their economic condition, keen intellect, or humble birth. Success is determined by their attitude, and persistence is the key. Thanks, Dr. Lee, for your delightful book that demonstrates this fact so vividly."

—Colonel Clarence R. (Reggie) Williams, USAF (retired)

"*Persist*—a daunting word for many, but an apt title for a book and the practical wisdom written within it. Dr. Lee lays out practical and pragmatic steps for anyone seeking to grow beyond their current position. What makes the book special, however, is that Dr. Lee painstakingly destroys the myth of complexity surrounding the barriers that we all encounter in our lives. He reveals the truth that most things really are pretty simple, just not always easy! We all have dreams, and Dr. Lee is spot on when he says 'The "how-to" guide may not be created for your dream yet, but it only takes knowing the "next-step" to get started.' Dr. Lee is living proof of what he writes, and what he writes can help many others become living proof of what he knows!"

—Bo Carrington, president, BCA Executive Consultants

"Dr. Lee brings a unique mix of experiences to bear in this easily consumable manual addressing common excuses for quitting or not even starting. *Persist* is a beautiful prescription because it is a medicine so widely applicable, and we need to take it often. Persistence enables us to overcome the myriad of challenges we face along our journeys. Simply continuing to do the work and focusing on the work gives us immunity to the distractions. Our daily dose of persistence keeps us working harder, focusing longer, and inching closer to the finish line."

—Anthony Hylick, PhD, IBM computer scientist

"Dr. Lee, or Lil' Lee as I've referred to him from our days as high school basketball teammates, has developed through a life of hard work, persistence, and belief the first all-natural herbicide for the proverbial 'seed of doubt.' This book gives you the tools necessary to embark on the whirlwind journey to success. It takes you deep into the soul and heart of Dr. Lee, who is living proof that the things that want to make us quit are no match for the force within us all. The force that is designed to eradicate any notion of not continuing to move forward!"

—Daniel Watson, CEO, Beneva Mayweather Foods/Visions Enterprise, LLC

"*Persist* provides a dynamic interplay between setting a dream and making it a reality. It provides the tools and key strategies to make epic life change while empowering individuals to fulfill their fullest potential for lifelong success. This masterful piece of writing inspires and energizes the mind and heart to burst through life's challenges with excellence, stamina, and fortitude."

—Dr. Marcellene Watson-Derbigny, associate vice president for student retention and academic success, California State University, Sacramento

"We could all benefit from living a life of greater persistence. Dr. Lee injects truth where we often tell ourselves lies. His step-by-step peeling of the layers leaves no stone unturned and provides the reader with not only a method but also the motivation to move past the barriers blocking their dream life. He shares his experiences as proof that the prescription works."

—Hart Robinson, president, Memphis Boat Center

"I am so very proud of Dr. Clarence Marcus Lee Jr.! He has now done it again! This new work is indeed inspiring but also a handbook for achievement. It has a healthy dose of 'I know how you feel because I was there once,' coupled with advisement for moving beyond those places. Well worth your investment!"

—Loretta Williams Walker, PhD, CPC, assistant professor, Drexel Pathway to Medical School (DPMS) program director, MPowerMeCoach.com

"Dr. Lee has become perhaps the most anticipated speaker at our annual BOSS™ camps. His conversations with our youngsters are entertaining, informational and inspiring, as are the short motivational pieces he produces, which we share with our youngsters as part of our year-round engagement. Dr. Lee's mantra is that the platform and resources afforded athletes should be catalyst for education, influence, and uplift. And he passionately strives to make that a reality for the next generation of student athletes. I'm glad to see Dr. Lee sharing his wisdom, hope, and experience on the Rx for living the life of your dreams."
—Everett L. Glenn, Esq., pioneering sports attorney, founder and executive director of the BOSS™ Program

"Dr. Clarence has an ability to get us to believe in ourselves, to tie that belief to our highest ideals, and to inspire us to never give up on our life dreams. He shows us that once we put our excuses aside, we can achieve anything we put our minds to with persistence."
—Michael Pusey, MBE, founder and CEO of Peckham BMX Club, member of the Most Excellent Order of the British Empire

"Dr. Lee does it again! This time with the prescription on how to break through! A must-read for anyone looking for the proper dose of not only inspiration but more importantly the application and strategy behind what actually creates successful outcomes. Dr. Lee does an incredible job delivering what's needed strategically through key points, story, and experience in a practical, easy-to-digest manner. If you need to get past struggles or simply want to achieve higher levels of success and don't know what to do next, read *Persist*; you will break through."
—Ernesto Benavides, entrepreneur and best-selling author of *Proving You Possible* and *Fit Life*

"Dr. Lee has written a practical guide to help anyone break through excuses and create their vision. I have mentored several agents in my business that have eventually opened their own agencies. This book helps me guide and lead my team members that have bigger visions and hopes for entrepreneurship."
—Armando Trevino, State Farm insurance agent, 2016 Top 20 of 19,000 agents in USA

Also by Clarence Lee Jr.

Well, My Mom Says …: Stories of Persistence, Faith, and Action

*For Chenelle, Chanel, Marc, and Caleb,
the reason I persist.*

Contents

Introduction xvii

1   Fear 1
        I'm Scared.

2   Self-Doubt 11
        I Can't Do It.

3   Money 22
        I Don't Have Enough Money.

4   Time 32
        I Don't Have Enough Time.

5   Know-How 41
        I Don't Know How

6   Timing 51
        It's Not the Right Time.

7   Circumstances 61
        My Circumstance Won't Allow It.

8   Failure 71
        I've Tried and Failed.

| 9 | Motivation | 80 |

I can't stay motivated.

| 10 | Comfort | 88 |

I'm Comfortable.

| Conclusion | 99 |

| Appendix   A Reader's Guide to Exercising Persistence | 103 |

| Acknowledgments | 113 |

| Notes | 115 |

| Author Bio | 121 |

Introduction

I headed out to the mailbox for the fifth week that summer, hoping for a different story this time. I had been working hard for years and figured today may be the day it would all pay off. As I approached the curb, I thought, *This could change it all.*

My routine had been to grab the mail and look through it quickly while still outside in the midsummer Kansas City heat. Once I found a few letters of interest, I separated them and placed them on top. I never opened them outside, just had them teed up for once I reached the door. This time I had several to open.

As soon as I broke the threshold of the door, I opened the first letter.

Dear Clarence,

Thank you for your application. Unfortunately ...

I never read past that word; I knew what was coming next. I blasted through the rejection letters one by one. I reset my enthusiasm with each letter, hoping the next one would be my chance. I had been applying to medical school for the past four years. I started applying when I was a junior in college, and now I was two years past graduation, with no real plan in sight.

My dream of becoming a doctor began in elementary school. I saw my mother put herself through nursing school, so she introduced me to the medical field early in life. She always told me I could do it. Now, after four years and hundreds of rejection letters, I was questioning if I had what it took.

This wasn't the first time I had faced adversity in my life, and it certainly wouldn't be the last. I'll jump to the end of the story; the next year, I made it into a postbaccalaureate program and eventually went on to graduate medical school. "Making myself a doctor" would set me up to accomplish many other things in my life.

When I walked across the stage and the presenter announced, "Dr. Clarence Marcus Lee Jr.," I knew in that moment I could do anything. I thought to myself that I had just made myself a doctor through pure effort and not giving up.

Well, Now Everything Was on the Table

How did I keep going after four years of rejection? How did I maintain enthusiasm and build the courage to try again each year? Of course, I thought about quitting many times. Why didn't I quit and try something else?

All of these questions will be answered in this book, but that's not all I want to accomplish. I'll share with you the prescription for living your dreams. I'll show you how, with hyperfocused effort, you can change your life.

Why *Persist*? And why now?

Part of the reason I wrote this book, is that as I grew up and watched people truck through life, I always wondered what their dreams were. My curiosity led me to ask many of them what they were excited about when they were young. Most would tell me about things they thought about as a child, like becoming a singer, an astronaut, a professional athlete, and so on.

Then, the conversation would shift. They would start to tell me the laundry list of things that happened in their lives that hindered them from pursuing their dreams. Many told me they had to grow up and find a "real job." Some told me they had kids. Others told me someone else took their chance. The list was endless.

I wondered to myself if that was going to be my path. Was I going to have a limiting story that I told *after* I talked about my childhood dreams? Was I going to have a reason for *not* living it?

How could I make my life different?

I want to approach this subject by addressing the top reasons people don't live their dreams. We'll go through them one by one, in hopes of removing one of these from the stories we tell ourselves about our journey. In today's world, most folks don't want to rock the boat. In other words, they are willing to stick with the status quo. Living your dreams is not the status quo; it is the exception. This book is for the people who want to be exceptional. We will need to break through the mold of the status quo to live our dreams, and here you will find tools that will help you accomplish just that.

Every chapter has lessons I learned the hard way and some that I learned from watching others. I am hoping these stories will lead you to take back some of your vision for your life. As I stated earlier, there is no lack of disempowering stories we tell ourselves. Everyone has a good one, but I'm going after one result in this book: crushing these excuses to allow every person to live a purpose-focused life. We will tackle every excuse with logic as well as practical exercise in the appendix that will help you grow and develop individually.

Purpose-focused living entails you waking up every day with passion, knowing that what you're going to do that day is the reason you exist. I don't want to offend anyone by making it seem that their story or circumstance is small, but if it's standing in the way of your dream, my goal is to help you remove it.

"Never permit a dichotomy to rule your life, a dichotomy in which you hate what you do so you can have pleasure in your spare time.

Look for a situation in which your work will give you as much happiness as your spare time."

—Pablo Picasso

As the title implies, I will be speaking mostly to your ability to persist in the face of adversity and circumstances. This, however, is not persisting simply for the sake of persisting. This persistence is based on you first identifying or reconnecting with your purpose in life. We are not called to persist in accomplishing the goals others have set before us. This would be the case if you are working in a job that you feel is unfulfilling. You are not called to persist in this effort.

Your life's purpose will call you to persist in your highest calling. Everything in this book is based in and highly targeted for use in *your* purpose. In order to persist, we need a compelling picture to go after and a "why" that is passion filled.

I started with the story of some of the things I had to go through to become a physician, but this book isn't about how to become a doctor. After finishing medical school and realizing everything was a true possibility for my life, I started to dream bigger. What if I ran the hospital? What if I was helping to make the policies? What if I didn't have to "go to work" every day? What if I didn't have a boss?

As I looked at the lives of physicians (specifically surgeons), I started to see things I wanted to change about that lifestyle. I trained in surgery, and the lifestyle my intern year was one I quickly realized wasn't for me.

So, as you pursue goals, you will also become more in touch with your purpose and your passions. I realized I loved medicine, but I didn't like the lifestyle that was laid out for me. Staying up all night, taking call, pagers at the dinner table—all this was not conducive to the life I wanted to create.

Life has an amazing journey component to it, and this journey is what we are called to persist through. My persistence in trying to get into medical school trained me that pure grit could get me anything in life. As I looked at other lifestyles and ways to contribute, I used the same mentality later to start companies and create value in a different way for people.

Now that I've clarified what we are persisting for and the value of the journey, it's time to live on purpose, and here's the prescription.

It's time to *persist*.

1

Fear

I'm Scared.

Our deepest fear is not that we are inadequate.
Our deepest fear is that we are powerful beyond measure.
Marianne Williamson

Fear is an interesting thing. It has the ability to erode our thinking and take it to a downward spiral very quickly. I like to talk about fear as an obsession of thought, because that's all it is; it is simply an obsession. Some may only associate the word *obsession* in conjunction with something that we long for very much. In a sense, fear is it's opposite. It's the obsession with and entrapment of our minds by the thoughts of what we incessantly *don't* want.

Think back to a fearful time in your life. You may remember a time when you were worried about something as an adult or a child. What was going on at the time? What were you afraid of? Something that was going to happen in the future, I'd venture. How likely was it that your fear would be realized?

Now, before I move forward, let's discuss some of the origins of fear and how it actually used to help us survive.

Back in the early ages of the cave dweller, humans had to fend for themselves against every creature in the wild. Attention to detail when it came to a potential predator was extremely useful. If they didn't properly react to a feeling of fear when a tiger was in front of them, well, they were no more.

I'm not talking about this type of fear. Let's just call that protective fear. That's the fear you feel when you're walking too close to a cliff or you are in the street and a car is coming right at you at one hundred miles per hour. Listening to and reacting to this type of protective fear when you are in physical danger is good. The fear that keeps us from living our dreams is a bit different.[1]

The fear I'm talking about is the type that can hold us back from going after what we want in life—the fear that is the slick opponent to living your dreams; the type that has very powerful effects when left to run wild in our brains. How does this fear keep us from our dreams? The short answer is *inaction*, but let me go a bit deeper into the tactics fear uses against us.

Fear of Rejection

We all long for acceptance in life. We all want to belong and to be a part of a group. The groups people want to be a part of may vary, but everyone wants to belong.[2] Fear of rejection has the ability to consume our brains with the storyline that if we take a chance, we will face painful rejection. This is very common for single folks on the dating scene.

Here's how a typical scenario plays out. A guy is very much interested in another person, but he isn't sure if she is interested in him. He goes round and round in his head about what to say, if he should say it, or how to say it. Until the thought of rejection creeps in.

What if she laughs in my face? What it she thinks I'm desperate? What if she tells her friends about how she dissed me? No one wants to bruise his or her ego like that; no one wants to feel the pain of rejection.

Remember, rejection isn't the only option. There is also the option that the other person may be interested in you as well. She may tell you she was just as fearful. She may even thank you for having the courage to come over. There's always two sides to the "What could happen?" question. The ability for us to move forward despite fear depends on whether we're disciplined enough to train our brains to truly consider both sides.

Fear of Failure

I've dedicated an entire chapter later on (chapter 8) to the topic of failure and how we use it as a reason for not living our dreams. Here I want to discuss how the *fear of failure* keeps us from taking action. Without action, we don't give ourselves a chance to fail. That is the power of fear, its ability to keep us frozen and terrified.

Failure also hurts. It is painful, just as much as rejection. No one would sign up willingly to fail. After reading this book, I'd like everyone to fail and to fail often, because it is in failure that we grow the most, and it is where we truly push ourselves. I'll go deeper into this in chapter 8.

Have you ever found yourself worried about failing *before* you try something new? Is the thought of failing more powerful than the thought of succeeding?

The best exercise I've read about and practiced when it comes to overcoming fear is one where you are asked to write out completely what your ultimate fear would look like.[3] So, say in the case of applying for a job, your fear is that you will be rejected. What is the worst thing that could happen?

Well, let's see:

1. You don't get the job.
2. You get laughed at.

3. Your boss demotes you for even asking for a different job.
4. The employer blacklists you, and no one else will ever hire you.
5. You're listed on a "got rejected" list.
6. You lose your job and don't get hired ever again.
7. You then lose your house and become homeless.
8. You're left to eat food out of the trash to survive.

Now, after you delineate what your worst fear looks like or what your worst day looks like, let's consider the odds of all this happening. How likely is it that you'll get rejected? Well, we can calculate that if you know the number of applicants and positions available. What about all the other things that crossed your mind? How likely are they?

After intense evaluation, you'll find that your worst fears are, for the most part, very unlikely. Honestly, the worst thing that happens (most of the time) is that you don't get the job and you go back to your current life.

The thing is, we miss out on ever trying because the fear of failure gets in our way, which means we won't take the risk of having something great happen. Instead we take the guarantee that our life will stay the same. *Huh?* Exactly! Doesn't make much sense when we put it that way, does it? But we do it all the time.

Fear of Embarrassment

Embarrassment can be one of the toughest things to deal with, especially when it's public. Taking a risk or going for our dreams can expose us to potential embarrassment. Our peers may see us fail as we attempt to achieve new things. They may ridicule us if we share our dreams with them. They may tell others that we're crazy for believing or trying something.

The opinion of our peers, family, and friends is valuable, but it can become restrictive when we place too much emphasis on what others think of us. I know you may be thinking, *Well, my friends matter to me, and my family has my back*. They are important, and they are in your corner, but they may not always see your vision for themselves. They may have a hard time seeing what you see in those moments. You can't worry about their belief. In those moments, it's time to lean on your inner beliefs.

So, I'm saying risk embarrassment and go after your dreams. What about the pain that could come if you fail? Think of it like this: the reward must be worth the risk. In other words, make sure you are dreaming big enough to make the risk of embarrassment worth it.[4]

Actions come with risk. The only way to avoid risk is to do nothing, and doing nothing isn't the recipe that will get you your dreams. We must be willing to stick our necks out and risk embarrassment before we can manifest our vision for ourselves.

One of the best exercises I have learned on the subject involves creating a fear curriculum. This involves writing down the things that you fear and putting a list of tasks in place that will help you overcome that fear. This is particularly effective when it comes to fear of embarrassment. If you are worried about what people think, line up activities that will require you to ignore others.

One great example is to sing out loud in public. Many people are afraid of singing in public, so the next time you are in a coffee shop or store, just start singing. Many people may look at you funny, but complete the verse and go about your day. Don't give an explanation for why you were singing; just sing a verse and quit. You can also do the same thing with dancing. Just break out in your best dance move while you're in line next. Work it out, and then just stop and go on about your business.

Absorb the uncomfortable feeling of the stares, but keep going. This will build your threshold for embarrassment. You're not harming anyone by dancing; the wilder the dance moves, the better. At best, you'll get a few laughs and feel good about it afterward.

CLARENCE M. LEE, JR. MD, MBA

Moving Past Fear and Taking Action

Our actions day to day are based in our highest beliefs. Just think about it: we move in expectation (belief) in everything we do. One of the examples I use when I illustrate this point during talks is sitting in a chair. When we believe in our minds that a chair can and will hold us, what do we do when we get ready to sit down?

We completely let go.

We drop into that chair like a weight on a fishing line in water. We don't hesitate. We don't put one leg in the chair or check its sturdiness with our hands first. We just plop down into it and let fate be what it may.

This is what expectation looks like, and it runs all of our actions. Now, is it possible that the legs of the chair could break? Is it possible that the back could fall off? Is it possible the chair could slide out from under you? Yes, these things are possible, but we don't really consider them as true alternatives. Instead, we act based in our belief that the chair will hold us. So, we sit down and don't think twice about it.

Throughout our day, we have to make hundreds, if not thousands, of little choices based in belief. Do I step into the street when the crosswalk sign says *walk*? Do I enter the intersection when the light turns green? Do I eat this food I just purchased at the store? It won't harm me, will it? Our expectations run our actions.

High Belief: My job will pay me.
Action: I go to work every day I'm scheduled to be there.
Low Belief: I can't make a living pursuing my passions.
Action: I procrastinate and put other things first.

Now, when it comes to living our dreams, we may not look at things in an expectation context. We consider the odds of an alternative quite often. There is much debate about why this is, but that's not my goal with this book. I want to increase that fire in you that says *I can create what I want with my life, and that is exactly what I will do.*

To overcome fear, we must address our expectations. What do we most believe about a potential course of action in our lives? Do we believe the likelihood of what we want to happen is high, or do we think it is more likely that what we don't want will happen? This is a fundamental question, and we all must be honest with ourselves. Exactly what do we believe?

Changing Our Thinking

Once you have given yourself an honest answer, you must then decide if you need to change the story you are telling yourself. One characteristic of fear is that it loves to replay bad screenplays in our minds.[5] It happens naturally if we aren't intentional about our thoughts. The next time you are fearful of something, count how many times you play out the scene in your mind. To counter the autoplay of worry, we must create and visualize, just as often, what we want to happen.

This takes practice and focus, but it can be developed in anyone. Instead of allowing the negative scene to play in your mind, you must change the script and make the movie in your head go the way you want. It may not be believable at first, but that is not the goal of this exercise. The exercise is intended to get you to become more aware of and intentional about your thoughts.

By executing this exercise we begin to visualize our dreams daily and counter the disbelief and fear that is rooted in our minds. This eventually, with time in practice, starts to influence our deepest beliefs. It helps us to increase the time we spend thinking about ways we can create our dreams, rather than ruminating about our fears.

Once we build our belief, we can build an action plan based around that belief. If we don't build our dreams, no one will. No one will tap you on the shoulder and say, "You know what? It's time for you to live your dreams. You now have permission."

You may say, *Yeah, right, man. All I have to do is intentionally think about what I want, and everything will happen for me?* Everything will *not* happen magically, but this thought process starts momentum that began with thought and eventually ends in action. These actions that are fueled by your belief lead to results that are aligned with your vision.[6] It all starts with the thoughts we hold. If we can't get ourselves to believe that our action will bring us results, it will be very difficult to convince our bodies to move to create it.

Where does fear camp out in your brain? What has fear kept you from doing? What have you worried about in the last week? Have you played out a negative scene in your head this week? Did you counter it?

These are the questions you will eventually ingrain in your spirit, to help you stay on top of your thinking. No thought gets to stay in your mind if it doesn't serve you or your dream.

In taking more action, we will also face more challenges. If we are to get to a place where we can overcome fear, we must learn to embrace challenges. The thing about challenges is that there is a huge unknown waiting for you. Will you be able to complete the challenge? How long will it take you? Some of these questions keep us from taking action. The fear of the unknown can leave you with many options to consider. Playing them all out in your head can be exhausting.

As stated earlier, there is always a possibility of something great coming from the unknown. It is this small switch in focus that can allow us to embrace challenges. More than likely, you've met someone in your life who really likes trying new things. It is also likely you've met people who are deeply afraid of change.

PERSIST

Fear of the unknown and not embracing challenges, although it may seem logical at the time, can lead you to live a life devoid of your dreams. Your life will test you in all of your weakest areas, and you will be required to pass these tests in order to fulfill your purpose. This will require you to be willing to embrace challenges and change.

If you are ready to overcome fear, you must:

1. 1. Correct fear-based thinking
2. 2. Act based off of your highest belief and not your greatest fear
3. 3. Embrace the difficulties that come with challenges and change

The final step in overcoming fear is taking action. Since fear's greatest victory is keeping us frozen in inaction, we must dedicate ourselves to taking action. There are many ways we can incorporate a "taking action" attitude for our lives, and I'll share a few of them with you here.

Taking action will lead to results. It doesn't matter what the initial results are; the point is to take action and create a result. Action occurs in a trial-and-error fashion, and I want to reiterate that this is not only about desired results. It's really about getting ourselves to take action when we have a challenge in front of us. Acting in the face of a challenge helps us to get over our fear of an undesirable result. When we take action, we focus on creating something new. That's the idea, getting used to creating things with your actions.

One thing I learned from my virtual mentor, Tony Robbins, is that taking massive action is one of the best ways to bring about change in your life.[7] Now it's time for us to take massive action, and we can start with making a list of any- and everything that could help us live our dreams.

Many people have a problem with this exercise because they overthink it. When you make this list, do not focus on what is *likely* to work. The only criterion is that it *could* possibly help us. That is it. Every thought that comes to mind, write it down. Our minds may tell us, *No, that won't work*, but write it down anyway. We'll work on the execution later.

Overcome Fear with Action

Getting ourselves to take action can be tough, but with this, we will build courage, and it will take courage to live your dream. As we act, we embrace challenge and welcome growth into our lives. I have a major bias toward action, because inaction is one of the most common reasons people don't live their dreams.

Again, as you start to envision what these actions will look like, remember to go back to the main components of fear. Are any of these fear tactics resurfacing? As you think about taking action, do you think about the opinions of others? This can slow you down. Dismiss this thought. Your vision is worth taking risks, and it is worth sticking your neck out.

People will judge you, no matter what you do, so focus your actions on your dreams. Let people judge you for chasing your dreams, not for living someone else's.

Beat: *I'm Scared*

Start: Developing courage and taking action

2

Self-Doubt

I Can't Do It.

Our doubts are traitors, and make us lose the good
we oft might win, by fearing to attempt.
—William Shakespeare

Before I get into the topic of self-doubt, I must call on the leading inner beast that attacks us in this area: the feeling that you are not worthy of the life you want.

We each have been raised in different environments and have adapted thought processes from our parents and our surroundings. One of the first things we must contemplate is our inner sense of what we are worth and what we are worthy of.

When I was growing up, many people talked about folks with money like they were evil and didn't care about the little guy. When they spoke of rich folks (granted, we didn't know many), they always spoke negatively, using comments like, "Well, they don't get it. They've got money," or "What have they been through? They've always had a silver spoon in their mouths."

This position on wealth inherently made me disagree with it. Without even knowing it, by entertaining these thoughts, I was sabotaging my own efforts to be rich one day.[1] This was just one example of an adapted thought process that pertained to money. There are many other areas in which we have an unconscious position that may be holding us back from our dreams.

The question I want you to ask yourself is, "What is the life I am truly worthy of?" Many of you started to get tripped up when I mentioned being worthy of *anything*. Especially being Christian, many believe we aren't necessarily worthy of a blessing, because we are sinners and it is through God's grace that we receive. I totally agree with this, but my faith also tells me I am a child of the King, and he is my heavenly Father. Because of that, I am entitled to an inheritance.

It simply becomes a question of one's focus. That is what determines your attitude and actions. If you focus on the fact that you deserve an inheritance, you will walk with that in mind. If you believe you are to do good with your blessing, you will walk with that in mind as well. It's all about your focus. In this case, the focus of *I'm worthy and meant to do good with my success* will lead a person to act completely differently than someone who believes he or she isn't worthy of success.

I am not in any way implying one person is better than another; I only mention this to help some see past the opposition that my rise up inside you when someone talks about being worthy. Feeling you are worthy doesn't oppose humility. You can move boldly in the direction of your dreams without being prideful or dismissive of other people.

We live in a world that implies the "worthy" term all the time. We may not hear it, but as an American, it is ingrained in our constitution. We don't say *worthy*, however; instead we call them *rights*. You can look at worthiness in a similar light. What rights do you feel you are entitled to in life? Do you believe it is your right to pursue your dreams? Do you think everyone on earth has that right?

PERSIST

When I start to ask these questions, people typically answer *yes*, and in that *yes* we now have to give ourselves permission to exercise those rights. By taking yourself through this mental exercise, you help to bring awareness to your deepest beliefs. This is where most of the work of this book is done—the path to becoming more aware.

By embracing the idea that we are worthy of the success we dream of, we make room to take more targeted action. Distance yourself from any thoughts of unworthiness. You are worthy of everything you imagine, and as you do the work it takes to get there, you will grow more confident in this truth. I'll talk about building confidence later on in the chapter.

Self-esteem can be seen side by side with the concept of worthiness, so I want to touch on this for a moment. Self-esteem can be defined as how you feel about your worth as a person—your life, your time, your presence and contribution to the world. How do you feel about *you*?

Self-esteem, in its purest form, should be rooted in your belief that every person has worth and the ability to contribute. This can easily be seen when it comes to others we watch in our lives. We see them doing big things and say to ourselves, *Well, this person has worth and is worth something.*

Worth is not monetary in this definition; it is your inner beliefs about yourself and your inherent worth, irrespective of possessions. Self-esteem isn't about what you can do, what you have, or where you're from. It's about how you feel when you look at yourself in the mirror.

As we begin to build our thought process through the practices of this book, we must start to raise the bar on our inherent worth. To believe you are worthy of your dream life, you must believe you have inherent worth. This sense of self-worth is critical, because as you charge forward toward your dream, you will need internal fortitude to withstand external obstacles. To persist after failure or disappointment, you must believe you have worth that isn't attached to a result or an outcome. It is *who* you are. It is how you see yourself.

But why do we doubt ourselves in the first place?

Comparisons

Self-doubt can also be triggered through comparison. As we begin to look around and measure the success of others and compare it to our own, we may begin to get discouraged.[2] We may see someone else who is living his or her dreams, and instead of becoming motivated by that sight, we get down on ourselves for where we are. We entertain thoughts that we will never get there—that they have an advantage. We start to build a case against ourselves as to why we can't have the same things.

Each person has his or her own struggles in life. From the outside looking in, we may not always share the complete perspective of others. In fact, it will be very hard to share others' perspective, not being them. One of the things I love about life is that we as individuals are all unique. Inherently, we all have unique qualities to bring to the world.

Your path may not be exactly like someone else's, but your journey is for you to tell. It allows you to be uniquely positioned to tell your story, to be the expert in your life.[3] Your walk is worthy of being told and watched as well. Everyone has to start from somewhere, and the somewhere you started from is the reason your story is interesting.

This works in several scenarios. I had the pleasure of meeting a young man a few months back, and as we got to talking, he told me how he had grown up wealthy and how his family had lost it all. He knew a little bit about my story and said, "Well, I didn't come from the inner city, but ..." I stopped him right there and told him that his story had just as much value as mine. Just because we came from different places didn't mean one was more worthy of being told.

If you have been on top and are now working your way back, your self-doubt can hold you back. If you are like I was (simply trying to get on the field to see the top), your journey is valuable as well. We all must remain humble, but don't downplay the things in your life you have overcome. A victory is a victory and worthy of celebrating. In our struggles, we gain better clarity of what it takes to overcome. It is this expertise that allows us to add unique value to the world.

Don't sit and look at a successful person and say, "That will never be me." That person has his or her own struggles you may not be aware of, and quite frankly, you may not want those problems! If you are going to compare, make sure you are fair about it. What do I mean by that?

Use the fair comparison rule—don't just compare yourself to those who have more; also compare to those who aren't as far along as you. Look at those who are less fortunate than you, and see how blessed you are. Comparison can be helpful if used to build our perspective. It can be destructive, however, when used as evidence against our own abilities.

Imposter Syndrome

I remember, upon getting into medical school, for the first week or so, all I could think about was whether everyone else thought I was smart or not. Were they going to know I got in through a postbaccalaureate program? Were they going to figure out how hard it was for me to get in? Would they think I wasn't smart enough and that I didn't belong?

The imposter syndrome or phenomenon is the feeling that you are acting like something you are not or you are among people who will find out you don't really belong in the group.[4] Many people suffer from this type of thinking. This phenomenon can lead to self-doubt if not recognized for what it is. These feelings occur naturally in many people and are not the identifier of a true imposter.

As you advance in life, you may run into these feelings, especially if you are going outside of the box and trying something new—something no one you know has done. It can be even stronger when you compare yourself to the past results of people in your family. We draw a strong identity with family, but if going outside of your family norm makes you feel like an imposter, fret not! You are not alone in this feeling. Remember, it is just a feeling; it is not the truth.

Naysayers

Another thing that fuels self-doubt is the opinion of others. Our brains seem to have a bias toward emphasizing negative things we hear.[5] In my life, I have come up against many people who didn't believe I could do what I told them I could do. Believe it or not, this initial doubt played a significant role in my life. In that moment, I had to take a position on how I believed. Did I agree with the naysayer who said I couldn't do it, or did I disagree? Do I allow this negativity to stick around in my brain, or do I replace it with a higher belief?

Naysayers aren't always trying to be harmful with their advice. Some of them truly don't believe you can do what you say you can. I remember when I was in college, one of my guidance counselors told me I shouldn't apply to medical school. Granted, I didn't have the best GPA. I had fallen asleep in her class many times. I was a basketball jock and missed class quite a bit for sports. Who was I to think anyone in their right mind would let me into medical school?

Looking back, I understand now where the "advice" was coming from. I could have just taken that advice and decided to pursue something else. Instead, I took that guidance and used it as fuel for my efforts in becoming a physician. It would be nice to have the support of everyone in our immediate surroundings, but that isn't always available. Don't let this be the reason you decide to do something else. Living your dream isn't about proving others wrong; it's about proving yourself right.

PERSIST

Naysayers have enormous power when you internalize true consideration of their words. This is the reason I wanted to include these thoughts in this chapter. Ultimately, they lead you to believe you aren't capable. They introduce a seed of doubt into your vision and plant it deep inside of you. Please be aware that naysayers are plentiful, but there are also just as many people who will encourage you. Don't let the few naysayers deter you. See them coming a mile away, thank them for their advice, and keep moving.

"Thank you, but no thanks. I know what I'm capable of, even if you can't see it yourself."

This is the highest truth. Try this one on for size. It fits you well.

Belief

We all have a choice in the thoughts we believe. We must begin to take ownership of this today. If your belief is holding your back, there are several things you can do to address this, the first of which is something I started practicing when I was in high school: verbal affirmations.

Using your voice purposefully to convince yourself is powerful. Take some time out and contemplate the opposite of the limiting thought you are holding. If you are telling yourself you cannot do it, take a moment and write down that you can. After putting it on paper, speak the thought out loud. Yes, tell yourself you can do it.

This practice is known to many as auto-suggestion and was popularized by the phenomenal author Napoleon Hill.[6] This is a learned skill and must be practiced before it is fully adopted. When you first begin, you may say to yourself, *This is stupid. Why am I speaking to myself?* Here is the deal: by speaking to yourself, you begin to hear the very thing that will help you.

When you encourage yourself, you take power into your own hands. By being intentional with our words, we can use the action of speaking and the influence of our voice to change the way we think and believe. It may sound silly, but this is a tried-and-true practice throughout history. It has been used for years, by many of the highest performers in the world.

If you aren't willing to speak to yourself in the positive, start by simply refusing to speak the thought that is holding you back. This can build momentum as you work on your thoughts with the exercises from chapter 1. Combining the thought work with intentional use of words—or intentionally not using words—can transform your thoughts and language.

Another practice is to visualize yourself winning before it happens. If you aren't sure how to get something done, don't worry; visualize anyway. This isn't always the easiest thing to do. It may be a stretch in your mind to even envision yourself at the top. Again, this is something that will take practice, but through proper visualization, you're able to see yourself there as you prepare. It's preparation that leads to the confidence that you can get things done. As I mentioned earlier, your feelings of worth (self-esteem) play a big role, but your ability to believe it is possible for you (self-efficacy) plays an even bigger role.[7]

Confidence

I can't conclude this discussion on self-doubt without including one thing that has helped counter the doubt in us all. Confidence has led many people to stick their necks out and go for it. Believing in you is the remedy for self-doubt. I want to discuss ways to build confidence, because it may not be inherent in everyone, but it doesn't matter, because it can be cultivated.

The funny thing about confidence it that internally we use our past victories to fuel our confidence. These past victories can be in any area. Confidence says, "I've overcome obstacles before; this one will be no different." How do we build up our record of victories?

Small goals and momentum.[8]

When I was playing basketball in high school and college, I was known for shooting three-pointers. I loved it when the announcer at the game would say, "Lee for three!" It became a nickname of sorts. When I was playing, I was a streaky shooter. I could hit ten three-pointers in one game and then come back the next game and hit one. One thing I learned in college was that confidence placed in the wrong areas can actually hurt your performance.

I don't want folks to think I am encouraging individuals to become conceited, because this is far from what I am teaching. In college, after I had a great game, I would have thoughts about how great I was. I would think, *Man, you're good. You're awesome!* This thought would return over the next few days when it was time for me to go to the gym and put up shots in my spare time. *You're awesome. Why do you need to shoot all these shots? You just hit ten threes last game.* There were many times when my past success, the very thing that fueled my confidence, actually caused me to set myself up to perform poorly.

Confidence is found and rooted in your preparation.

If you are trying to build confidence in any area of your life, this basic lesson is very powerful. Preparation is key for confidence in anything. You must spend the time preparing in order to place yourself in the best position to perform the way you know you can. When I was listening to the "you are great" voices in my head, I was placing my confidence in me or who I was, not in my work ethic. This was a mistake.

My work ethic is what got me to the point where I could shoot like that. It was the routine of going to the gym that made the shots feel comfortable. It was the hours missing and missing that allowed me to continue to make adjustments and improve my shooting technique and form. When I stopped my preparation, my performance always dropped. It would sometimes take me two or three games to wake up and realize I needed to get back in the gym and put more shots up.

The same was true in an academic setting. The more time I spent preparing for a test, the more confident I was going into the exam, and the better I did. In contrast, in times when I did not prepare, I was afraid and timid going into the exam, because I knew I hadn't put everything I had into it. I knew there was more I could have done.

For each person, this will be different. Some folks I went to medical school with never thought they had done enough before an exam, even though they had put in more time than any of us—so this concept can also be overdone. Your confidence should lie in your ability to try, to act, and to exert effort, enhancing your ability to improve. Only you know what you are capable of, so you're the ultimate judge of effort. You're the competitor you're playing against. Give your all, but at the end of the day, only you will know if you gave your best. If you're giving your all and have done all you can do, then you can rest assured that your confidence is well deserved.

As you prepare daily, set the bar as high as possible. To stay with the basketball analogy, when I was shooting free throws, I never shot just three or four at a time. I would shoot one hundred at a time. I would never shoot one hundred free throws in a row in a game, but I set the bar higher for practice, because by the time I was in the game and had to shoot two, I was used to making twenty in a row, so I was prepared and confident that I could make two.

Confidence is not a "can I or can't I do it" thing. It's an "I'm going to do what I've trained myself to do" thing.

When you have this mentality that you are preparing for performance that is rehearsed, you place your emphasis on preparing. You can't expect to produce in real life what you haven't produced in practice. I am really driving home this preparation idea because I want us all to understand it's about being confident that you can do *what you've done* in practice.

So, understand that you are worthy, stop the comparisons, mute the naysayers, and override the imposter syndrome. Build your belief with auto-suggestion, and solidify confidence through dedicated practice. You've got what it takes.

Beat: *I Can't Do It*

Start: Building self-esteem, belief, and confidence

3

Money

I Don't Have Enough Money.

Chase the vision, not the money; the money will
end up following you.
—Tony Hsieh

This idea that it takes money to live your dreams has stopped people dead in their tracks for decades. I want to attack this misconception from many angles, but let's start with discussing this idea of value.

Bringing Value

When I look at money, all I see is a medium that is exchanged for something else of value. When we go to the store and see something we want, we have to make a decision. Is it worth what the store is asking for it? If we feel it is, we'll fork over the cash or charge it on our credit card. We are exchanging the valuable dollar for the product we want: TV, computer, shoes, clothes, etc. This is how a consumer thinks: *I want this; what am I willing to pay for it?*

The store, on the other hand, thinks a little bit differently. They think, *What can I add to the marketplace that has value? What can I sell it for?* The exchange of cash is based on someone bringing value to the table. In the case of entrepreneurs and employees, they think of bringing value to the market in many ways. The entrepreneur thinks like the store, but the employee thinks of things in terms of what type of service he or she can provide a business. What position can they bring value to, or where can they fit into the structure of the organization?

When it comes to bringing value, we've all done this if we've ever had a job. You have provided a company with your service (value) in exchange for a salary. In the case of living your dreams, it is simply the concept of bringing value. You don't need money to bring value. Just like you don't need money to apply for a job, you just need to be able to work. If you're able to work, you're able to create your dreams.

Granted, you may be able to see how you can bring value to the marketplace, but you get stuck in the grandiose vision of how it needs to be done. You will need money for this grandiose vision, but you don't need money to start to bring value. If we can put down our grand view of how it needs to be done, we can use our brainpower to consider how it can be done with little money.

Think of your dream in the sense of how you can live it now, not what you'll need to live it. As long as you lack, you'll stall on your vision.

Creating Value

Entrepreneurs since the beginning of time have figured out ways to create value out of thin air. Value is relative to need, and needs are mostly based around problems. If you are able to identify a problem and provide a solution, you have just created value.

The problem-solving focus is just one way to create value; you can also create value by providing a unique experience, sharing your expertise, or showcasing your talents, whatever they may be. To create value, your only limit is how creative you can be with ways to bring it.

Yes, companies eventually spend a lot of money, but this is once there is a necessity to spend. Once a company has gotten to a certain level, they must spend money to scale their business. Basically, they'll spend money with the hopes of creating more value and making more profit. This scaling process can take place after the concept or idea of a business has been proven in the marketplace. In other words, once you've sold so many you can't keep up with the orders, now you may need money or to hire help to grow the business further.[1]

Communicating Value

Along with bringing and creating value, one must also be able to communicate what that value is. After you have identified your positioning in the market, you must now be able to sell this idea.

How do you communicate to others your brilliant value-creation strategy? I stated earlier that when it comes to successful businesses, most of them are addressing some problem a person has. These problems could be as simple as needing a car to get to work or more complex like how to save my money pretax and lower the tax burden.

I know I may sound like Business 101 here, so if your dream doesn't involve running a business, but you still feel like your lack of money is stopping you, I'll get to you next. Bear with me.

Communicating value is a skill that all successful entrepreneurs possess. Your ability to identify a problem and articulate to a customer how you can solve that problem faster, cheaper, or easier is critical in acquiring their patronage. I am a huge proponent of sales training. When I was in high school and college, I had several jobs where I had to sell things. My first sales job was selling shoes in the mall. I'll never forget this job, because after I realized how to sell, it was the easiest job ever!

I naturally love to talk to people, so that was never a problem. Getting them to buy from me was an issue in the beginning. I first needed to learn how to build rapport quickly. How do I get them to understand I want to help them and not just sell them something? It took me a few weeks to get the hang of it, but my strategy was to engage them in conversation first. After I would talk to them a bit, I would start asking questions about why they were in the store. Using great listening skills, I'd learn exactly what they were looking for or what they had come to buy.[2]

The selling didn't stop there. Part of my job was to show the customers other things in the store I thought they would value. From the conversation, I would pick up clues on what types of things they were into, what their style was, etc. I studied what they were wearing, looking for clues to what their previous purchasing behavior was like. After using my listening skills and taking notes, I would show customers other things they might like. I loved the job, because many times the customers would celebrate with me after I showed them something. It was like high-five, man this is great!

As you ponder how you will communicate your value in the market, I'd stress the understanding of what problem you are solving and how you are smarter, better, faster, stronger, than others.

Business

The "I don't have money" excuse is most often used by someone who wants to run a brick-and-mortar business. Here are some examples from history where people with little to no money figured out how to add value anyway.

Facebook/Twitter/Napster/Instagram

I'm going to include all of these in the same section. I love all of their stories, and the tech world of Silicon Valley has built an amazing formula for creating billions out of thin air. All of these companies followed it to a T. The founders of these companies didn't start with millions; most of them had very little before their companies blew up.

Facebook took the world by storm in the early 2000s. They created a new way for people to connect online and build communities. All this took was an idea, some expertise in coding, and the ability to communicate how this was going to be huge to investors. Twitter did the same thing: created a cool website, made it free to use, built a user base, and then started to implement revenue-generating streams into the business. Now these websites and apps have become havens for targeted advertising, which I think is ingenious, by the way.

Nowadays, people can start websites with no money, at a public library on borrowed computers, and make millions. Many of these startup founders didn't have college degrees, but that didn't stop them. Money shouldn't stop you either.

Subway

Back in 1965, Fred Deluca had no cash to start a business. He knew he wanted his own sandwich shop and figured his best bet would be to get a loan from a friend. He took that loan and opened his first shop, worked his butt off, and now we have the worldwide corporation Subway. Here's an example of your ability to communicate the value to potential investors. No money was needed on Fred's part.

Spanx

Sara Blakely, with no money or prior patent knowledge, researched product patents and wrote her own. She discovered a gap in the market and wanted to offer women another option for undergarments.

She would go on to create Spanx. In the beginning, she would travel and do in-store demonstrations of her product for women. Talk about dedication! She did everything she could think of to make the product a success. When you have that type of dedication, you are destined to succeed.

She didn't let the fact that she couldn't afford to have a lawyer file for a patent or the fact that she knew nothing about hosiery manufacturing stop her. The first time I heard her story, I was so amazed, I went online to watch as many interviews with her as I could find. This is a great example of someone who found a problem to address with her product. She was a part of the target demographic for the product and had incredible insight into her ideal customer's psyche. That, my friends, is called expertise, and she capitalized on this by creating a product where she understood the end user's experience well.

She has now gone on to be one of the youngest female self-made billionaires in America.

Apple

I must admit, I am a superfan of Apple, as well as an investor in the company. This company and its legendary founder, Steve Jobs, is one of my favorite stories of regular folks creating a life and business that has changed the world.[3] Steve Jobs and his partner started creating computers in their garage. They cold called their first customer and closed the deal before they even had the product! They believed in their product so much they were willing to stick their necks out and dedicate their time to making it a success.

To say they have revolutionized personal computing is an understatement. Apple also changed how most of the world consumes music. They are an example of company that wasn't willing to settle after having one success, but an organization that was constantly looking for ways to add value to the world.

Just in case I haven't convinced you that you can start a megabusiness with little to nothing, in this next section, I'm going to highlight some of my favorite individual rags-to-riches stories.

Oprah

I think my absolute favorite billionaire who came from nothing is Oprah Winfrey. She continues to be an inspiration to me to this day, but reading her story is absolutely mind-blowing. To say she came from humble beginnings is an understatement, but we all had to start somewhere, right? Oprah took what she had (a knack for finding stories and doing great interviews) and ran with it.

Starting off doing news in high school led her to attend college as a communications major. She later got a job hosting a low-rating morning talk show. Through her vision in herself and her belief she worked to make that show number one. The rest is history. She took her interest and expertise and created a billion-dollar empire.

Ralph Lauren

I've always loved Ralph Lauren's clothing and design. Being one of the biggest names in American apparel, he's built quite an empire for himself. I love his story because he was actually working for a large clothing retailer and had a few ideas for furthering their line. These ideas weren't exactly welcomed or embraced.

Instead of letting his dream stop there, Ralph decided he was going to make his own ties and started selling them himself. He took his love for fashion and his ability to create compelling designs and built the many brands of Ralph Lauren that we know today.

The thing I love about his story is that he didn't wait for someone to give him permission to be a fashion mogul; he simply figured out how he could add value right then and there and did it! It's inspirational to hear these stories of determined and driven people taking action. I can only imagine what fearful thoughts he had to persist through. Because he was compliant with the persistence prescription, we now have awesome clothes to buy.

J. K. Rowling

I wanted to mention an author because as a writer you have to create and continue to write, big agent or not. Now enters J. K.; she was living in government housing and on welfare while she was writing *Harry Potter*. She was also a single mother. She accepted no excuses and continued to create. I will talk in chapter 7 about how some people use their circumstances as proof for why they *can't* live their dreams. J. K. finished the book, and the Harry Potter series went on to be an international bestseller. I'm thankful she continued to persist, even without money for a typewriter. I am not doing her story its true justice, just touching on a few things, but this is definitely one you need to read for yourself if you're looking for more motivation.

Mark Cuban

I picked up Mark Cuban's book *How to Win at the Sport of Business* a few years back, and he did an awesome job of telling his story. Talk about a hustler! I loved reading it, because it's proof that no matter what your background, if you're hungry enough, you can make it big.

After getting fired from a computer job, Mark went on to start his own company, competing with his former employer. He cold called and reached out to potential customers. He expressed the value he could add, he maximized relationships, and he got customers. He is now one of the world's few billionaires.[4]

The central idea is this: your dream isn't attached to something you have to acquire.

Start Small

If you're in a financial position where you think you need money to move forward, one helpful strategy is to think small. Many of us look at the big picture or the total amount needed and get discouraged. If you are $100,000 in debt and you only make $20,000 a year, it can be easy to get discouraged.

Always remember, when a goal seems too large to obtain, break it into small, digestible sections. Start by putting money away little by little. You may not think that a few bucks a month will get you far, but it adds up over time.

If you have to get a second job temporarily to save the money, do it. Suck it up and sacrifice the time and energy now for the big goal, but chip away at it little by little. Avoid feeling overwhelmed by focusing on small bits instead of the daunting whole. Always keep the mark in sight, but hyperfocus on the baby step to stay focused day in and day out.

One thing I've learned along the way is that you must sometimes be willing to do the things most people aren't willing to do, to live your financial dreams.[5] That can include things like living beneath your means for a period of time or sacrificing some luxuries while you are pursuing your goal.

Many of our luxuries are sucking our bank accounts dry, which leaves us with little to invest in our vision. For many, simply letting go of some of the name brands or conveniences will lead them to the money they are looking for.[6]

If you have a vision of starting a great company and you don't have a building, remember Apple started in a garage. You can start there too. Everything doesn't have to be perfect; you can improve along the way. The idea is not to quit, but keep going. If you're afraid to start, get started anyway!

PERSIST

As you may have picked up from the stories shared earlier, all of these entrepreneurs were resourceful; they looked for ways to get started right where they were. They didn't wait for the money, they didn't get too far ahead of themselves, they tried little by little, and eventually became that success.

Your dream is alive and well right inside of you; it is up to you to be creative enough to make it happen. If our focus is on what is standing in our way, we will always have something available to blame for our inaction or lack of results.

As we switch our focus to how we can live our dreams now, we spend more brainpower creating the life we want. Use your precious focus and brain energy on what will work for you, not what's working against you. In the case of believing you need money to live your dream, use all the energy and focus to ponder how you can live your dream now.

What can you do today that will bring you closer to your dream?

Beat: *I Don't Have Enough Money*

Start: Creating value now

4

Time

I Don't Have Enough Time.

> Time is a created thing. To say I don't have time is
> to say I don't want to.
> —Lao Tzu

It was 3:00 a.m., and I finally got to lie down. The old twin mattress I was on felt like it was purchased in the '80s. The fourth floor of the medical center had become my home. I was on my internal medicine rotation, and I hadn't slept in about forty hours. Pulling call was brutal, and I was the type who wanted to get things done, so that led to me staying a lot longer than I should some days.

As I lay looking at the ceiling that night, a simple question popped into my head: *What in the world am I doing?* I hadn't talked to my family in weeks. I hadn't seen my daughter in months. What was I working so hard for? I wanted to provide for my family, right? I wanted a better life; I wanted more for my daughter. My pursuit of this "better life" had taken me miles away from those I loved. It had taken the majority of my time and was now stealing my sleep as well.

I thought, *Is this all for me or for someone else?*

That night, I decided I would start to make time pursuing what I felt I was on earth to do. I thought and thought, and all I kept coming up with was that I needed to mentor young guys who were like me. I needed to share a positive message with people. I needed to go back to the neighborhoods I was from and talk to the young folks about their lives.

So I actually found my purpose by pursuing something else (medicine).

In that moment, I realized the deeper "why" behind my pursuits to become a physician. I wanted to be in a position where I could positively impact someone's life every day. I was working on a healthcare team and rendering patient care, but I wanted to speak to more than just their physical ailments. I wanted to speak to their lives. I wanted to inspire them.

(If you're struggling with finding your deeper "why," I created an online course to help you do just that. For more information on the Purpose-Focused Formula Course, *visit www.clarenceleejr.com/courses).*

With this new focus, I started a mentoring program at a local high school the next year. This mentoring led me to my first public-speaking opportunity, and from there I built CMLEEJR Companies, LLC. I continued in my medical training and completed an intern year in surgery; then I went on to serve in the USAF as a flight surgeon before I decided to split my time running my company and seeing patients part time.

Where is your time spent?

If you took an inventory of how you actually spend your time, how much of that time is spent chasing or creating your dream? Many folks say, "Well, the reason I can't spend time doing this is because I have to do other things to live."

Take a moment to look at your schedule from last week. How much time did you spend at work? How much time did you spend with your family? How much time did you spend sleeping?

Write it all out, and calculate the hours. If you have a traditional job that you aren't in love with, after you add up all the time you spend commuting and preparing for work, I'm sure this is the number-one thing on your list. Some would say that is normal. We have to work, right? The problem with this logic is that it leaves no time for us to create our dreams. We're too busy creating the dreams of other people.

If you work for someone else, there was an individual who decided he or she wanted to create a company that would one day employ others. That is the reason you have a job. Some person or people had a vision they were dedicated to creating, and they spent the time doing it. If you're working in a job you love, I'm not talking to you. If you have a job you feel you were put on earth to do, then good for you! I'm talking to the folks who are hoping to create a life where they spend the majority of their time doing what they love or working in the areas they are most passionate about.[1]

When you wake up, you must ask yourself, *Whose vision am I helping to actualize today*? When there are too many days in a row when that dream is the dream of someone else, it's time to dedicate more time to your vision.

Whose dream are you building?

We all need to ask ourselves this question frequently, because conventional advice suggests we get a great job and help build someone else's dream. Who has sold you the vision of their dream? Has the company you work for sold you their leadership's vision? I am only pointing this out because this is exactly what you have to do to get *your* vision out there. You have to sell your surroundings, your employer, and your family on your vision. You can do this in several ways, but the one thing that has to be there is consistency in the *time* you invest.

There are some great companies out there doing great work, but if you're reading this book, I'm fairly certain you're trying to figure out how you can persist in pursuing your dreams.

"When you find yourself on the side of the majority, it is time to pause and reflect."

—Mark Twain

I'm not against traditional jobs, but obviously I'm a proponent of the life of entrepreneurs. If your dream isn't to be an entrepreneur, the idea is to not settle for *less than* what you think you can contribute. If you have found yourself in a position where you aren't contributing to your highest potential, it's time to carve out time in your day to help you get there. This is even helpful if you've changed positions and want to do more.[2]

This time is used to move you intentionally in the direction of your dream. For the aspiring writer, this means spending time researching the book industry. This is spending time studying great authors and honing your skills. For the aspiring athlete, this is spending time in the gym or on the field working out every day. For the aspiring CEO, this is finding ways you can contribute in your current position and overdelivering on your current job description. Now a question still remains: how do you find more time?

Priority vs. Priorities

Your priority always gets done; everything else is explained away.

In life, we wear many hats, and this causes us, at times, to have competing priorities.[3] What are we serving at this time? What's top on our list today? We can find ourselves asking this question often.

What I'd like you to consider at this time is that at any time, there is only one top priority, and it's that priority that all other things are scheduled *around*.

What is this priority for you, and how do you figure it out? What's the first thing you think about in the morning? Better yet, why do you wake up at the time you do? Is this the time your job requires you to wake up, or is this the time you wake up because you're excited about what is to come during the day?

I'll take it a bit deeper. Whenever there is a significant event in your life or an event you really want to attend, what do you think about next? Is it how much leave or vacation time you have? Is it the work schedule? Are you trying to figure out how you can move things around in your schedule so you can make this happen?

When our job, or better yet, making money is the number-one priority in our lives, it's usually the first thing we consider when we need time for ourselves. When I asked the question earlier about how you are going to find time, did you think about your job?

Creating the life that we dream of includes having time to do the things that really matter to us. For me, that was spending time with my family. After having lived the extremes of not being in control of my time (because of military service and graduate medical training), I promised myself that I would only make decisions that were consistent with my top priority.

Our highest priority runs our lives; it's the center we always refer back to in times of decision. How will this affect our number-one priority?

Finding Time

As we pursue our dream life, we will need to free up time to do just that.[4] What does this look like to you? What can you start to do with a little as one hour a day? When you start to introduce this dream-chasing time, the best way to implement this is one hour at a time. Start to carve out thirty minutes if you don't think you can do an hour up front, but time must be set aside.

It's time to see how badly you really want this, and it's time to check your motivation. If you can't find an hour to dedicate to your dream, is it really your dream? Are you okay with not having this as a part of your life? If you die without having pursued it, how will you feel?

There is another tactic to use when you are trying to implement a new process into your life. In this case, we are talking about creating time that is blocked off to specifically be spent moving us closer to our dreams. You simply begin to schedule things around your dream-chasing time.

In most cases, what gets done is what everything else is scheduled around. In a sense, this is how most people identify priority number one. How do you use this idea in your favor when it comes to dream chasing? Schedule your dream chasing first!

Everything else gets put in the queue before time is spent on it.[5] I know this sounds simple, but it is a basic tactic that will ensure what is on the schedule gets done. This would mean when you are planning out your free time, dream chasing gets put in first, and then you work around it.

Most people understand this very easily when it comes to their work schedule. We've all heard someone say, "I can't. I'm working." This is the same thing, except you are protecting your time that is dedicated to working on your dream.

It Takes Time

The reality is, no one has ever become an expert or excellent at anything overnight. We have to spend time refining and honing our skills in our passion in order for them to work for us in the greatest way. I trained my intern year after medical school in surgery. I got to work with some amazing surgeons, and they all had similar advice when it came to learning a skill. We all have the ability to read and theorize about a concept, but it is in the practice of that skill that we become experts. There is no way around the work, and every surgeon I worked with told me to figure out more ways I could spend time refining my surgical skills.[6]

As I was trying to learn how to tie efficient knots in the operating room, one surgeon suggested I tie knots as I sat in traffic or while I rode the train. It was down time I would waste if I didn't have a plan of action to move me toward a goal.

Finding time is about making your vision a priority and scheduling around it. Until it becomes that important to you, it will remain just a dream.

Another example of when the "I don't have time" excuse gets in the way is going to the gym. As a physician, I have helped many people with their fitness goals. One of the first things I get off the table before I discuss anything else is how are they going to make time to do the work. If you haven't worked in a plan to actually get you to the gym or to keep you on track, it's not worth talking about yet.

"I don't have time" has kept people from going to the gym for decades, and it has led to many early deaths, trips to the emergency room, heart attacks, and strokes.[7] The workaholic says, "I have to take the case or this call. I have to be at this meeting or whatever." Everything is a "have to"; well, when you are finally ready to make your dream happen, it must become a "have to."

One of the things I've heard said before is that you need to turn your "shoulds" into "musts" in your life. The things you always tell yourself you should do, you now tell yourself you must do. It's a simple change in vocabulary, but when practiced, it can lead to revolutionary transformation. Think about it: when you *must* do something, what do you do? How do you view it? What are the stories you tell yourself? They are a whole lot different than the stories you tell yourself about the "shoulds" in your life, aren't they?

Our Connected World

Another exercise I'd like you to do is to calculate how much time you spend connecting with others online. Social media is a great thing, and I use it quite a bit myself, but this constant connectedness has its down side. In a sense, we are giving people all over the world direct connections to us 24/7. Many of us have our Twitter and Facebook notifications sent to our e-mail and phones. God forbid we miss a private message or a mention on our feed. Oh wait, someone just tagged me in a pic on Instagram!

Our ability to stay in contact with our loved ones and friends is great, and I applaud these companies for the business model they have created. So, while I love social media, I also love being productive and spending my time doing what I was meant to do. Having our social-media feeds at instant access every waking moment can create a never-ending appetite to stay connected. It creates this culture of "wait, I have a free second; let me check my Facebook."

When I hear people tell me they don't have time for their dreams, I ask them if they have any social-media profiles. Of course, most people will say yes. I then ask them to divert all of their social-media time into their dreams. Here's the number-one response I get: "Well, I'm not even on Facebook/Twitter/Instagram like that."

Okay, sure. Let's try to calculate the time we spend engulfed in our feeds, looking at pictures, liking statuses, or responding to messages. We all spend time doing this, but there is a time and place for everything.

As we try to find time for our dreams, we must look at all of our waking moments. We have plenty of areas where we can shave time; it's simply a matter of being creative as we look for that time. In this chapter, I have referenced several amazing resources for ideas on productivity and how to find more time in your day. Check the notes for a few books and articles that are must-reads on this topic.

Beat: *I Don't Have Enough Time*

Start: Turning your dream into a must and scheduling everything else around it

5

Know-How

I Don't Know How

> Knowing is not enough; we must apply. Willing is
> not enough; we must do.
> —Johann Wolfgang von Goethe

Many of us have the motivation and a vision we want for our lives but get stuck at the how-to stage of our action plan. We just don't know where to start. How do you build a million-dollar company? How do you become a platinum-selling recording artist? How do you make it to the pros?

We can find ourselves sitting, stuck in inaction, because we just don't have the plan. This holds many of us back. Our dreams are so large at times that putting a step-by-step guide together can be daunting.

I found myself in the same position as I began to realize I wanted to run my own company. I had similar questions about how other entrepreneurs did it. How small did they start? How long did it take them? Obviously, all of the other things I've discussed surfaced as well. Can I do this? Will I fail? How do I find the time?

Before I get to the nitty-gritty of what to do, I want to address several of the psychological hurdles that keep some people from ever taking the first step.

1. Believing in Luck

Obviously, every successful person must also be lucky, right? All of them have gotten a lucky break that has given them their shot, right? One of the first decisions that helped me move forward on my journey to create the life that I wanted was to rid my mind of the "luck" excuse. I mean, come on, we've all heard someone explain away the hard work of a successful person with the notion that they were lucky.

It usually goes something like this: "Yeah, well, they just got lucky. That could have been me." Yes, it could have been you, but it wasn't luck that got the person the results. When you accept luck as a reason for success, you completely take the hard work, dedication, and struggle out of the picture.[1]

An amazing thing happens when you start to realize that every successful person had to work to get there: you begin to appreciate the struggle they went through. I challenge you to ask people about their story when you admire their results. You will most likely be amazed by the things they had to do and go through to get to where they are. This appreciation for the struggle is a great starting place to start a conversation if you'd like to learn their story.

As I'll discuss shortly, finding a mentor is one of the strategies you can use to learn where to start. I don't know of any better way to start a mentoring conversation than to ask someone about his or her story. Showing appreciation will go a long way. This is only magnified when you have done some research and know a little bit about the person.

Luck is *not* the reason for success. There is such a thing as being in the right place at the right time, but the majority of the time, this is not driven by luck.

"I'm a great believer in luck, and I find the harder I work the more I have of it."
—Thomas Jefferson

As we prepare to live our dreams and begin to take action toward them, we will find ourselves in the right place more often than not. If you are mission driven and continuously looking for opportunities to expand your odds of success, massive action will serve you well. If I am in action mode, I'm researching conferences, going to seminars, and networking. All of these allow for more of an opportunity to have a big break or to make a great relationship.

I'm reminded of the story about the discovery of Justin Bieber. He was found after performing a song and posting the video online. After this video landed in the hands of some major folks in the industry, he was given a shot. Now, was that luck, or was that a result of him and his parents taking action? You cannot believe it was luck, but some will say, "Well, I posted a video, and I didn't get picked up by Usher." Your walk will not be identical to others', but I will reiterate it was his action that got him to the place to even be discovered. With no video online, maybe he isn't discovered, or maybe he takes another action, and that's the one that does it. Again, it's about taking action first.

Luck begins to show up after hard work has set its ground in your life. Believing luck comes from anywhere else will keep you in a place of disempowerment. In order to take action, we must feel empowered. We have already been given the power to act; now we must use our actions to create the things we want in our lives.

To move forward, we must let go of the thought that our lack of luck is the reason we aren't where we want to be in life. This realization paid huge dividends for me personally. Because once I let that mind-set go, I moved toward the real creator of luck: hard work. Let's create some luck by taking massive action.

2. Realistic Goals

Sometimes in our frustration in trying to find what to do, we do what we know how to do. What do I mean by this? We have all had examples set before us. They may have been chosen by you, but in most cases, the early influences in our lives weren't personally handpicked. These examples showed us a way; they showed us what worked for someone else. They showed us how someone else did it. When you know the blueprint for creating something in life, that vision or goal is more realistic to you.

Am I promoting creating a vision and going after it for your life? Yes, I am, but the goals that many of us set are realistic to us because that is all we know. Living *our* dream isn't necessarily realistic to us, but working the job one of our parents worked is. Many of us didn't have folks in our lives who were living their dreams, and thus we got the advice that we needed to find a good job or "do what I did." Why did we get this advice? Because that is what they did. It's the formula they knew.

In their attempts to provide good advice, they gave you a realistic goal, and as a result, many of us pursued something that was less than our vision for our lives. This dilemma of the realistic goal holds a lot of us back. My guidance counselor in college was giving me what she thought was good advice when she discouraged my attempts to attend medical school. She thought she was doing me a favor by telling me how it really was; to clue me in on how difficult it was to gain admission. She was helping me pick a more realistic goal. To her credit, she had been teaching for decades, and this experience had shown her what results someone with my GPA achieved—and medical school was not on that list.

Here are the problems with realistic goals: They don't require you to push yourself. They don't require you to act in faith. They don't take you through the struggle your true dream will provide. It's more of a cruise-control setting for life. Just follow this formula, and you'll be fine.

The thing is, our dream doesn't have an exact cookie-cutter recipe, and it requires us to travel in unchartered waters. Look at it this way: your story will be unique and will require you to step out on faith. This risk you take (walking in faith) is worth the massive reward of living your dream. It's simple risk and reward, but in the formula of life, your dream will require the most risk and the greatest ability to believe.[2] I will talk later in the chapter about finding examples to model. This is in the context that you are looking for people who are living the life you want, not following the advice of someone who doesn't have the results you want.

3. Thinking Small Keeps You Small

The third psychological barrier to getting started working toward your dream is thinking small. Similar to the "realistic goals" example, you can also make your vision smaller in an attempt to increase the odds of success. If we allow ourselves to shrink our dream because it scares us, we aren't giving ourselves a chance to get to create our ultimate life.[3]

Thinking small doesn't do you or anyone else a favor. It's a case of wasted potential. How will you ever know if you would have been able to do it if you change the goal? I liken it to starting out saying you're going to do something ten days in a row, and then, once you reach eight, changing the goal to eight days instead.

Throughout this book, I will be giving you the logic and mental edge to persist, but you must believe and follow the exercises along the way. By feeling empowered, we can convince ourselves that our actions are capable of creating the results we want. That is all we need, to persist in the thought pattern that our actions can create our vision.

So, now that we know luck enters into the equation after hard work and that our dream is our own and will require our greatest faith, it's time to get going.

So, where do I start?

In today's Information Age, and with access to the Internet, you can learn how to do almost anything. When people tell me they don't know where to start, I'll ask a simple question like, "Have you Googled it?" The reality is there is *some* information on everything on the Internet; it just requires a little digging. I'm not suggesting that all the advice you'll find on the Internet is worth following, but it is a worthwhile place to start. Some of the challenge will be sifting through everything you do find and pulling out the reputable things. This can be done through checking the sources and cross checking with people you trust.

When I was trying to figure out how one becomes a doctor, I went to Google and just started Googling. From there, I went to websites of medical schools and learned about their admission requirements. Then I looked at how to apply and found the site for the admissions exam (MCAT). All of this I found on my own at a public library. I also had my mother, who was in the medical field (working as a nurse), help me connect with doctors she worked with.

Talking It Up—Always Be Marketing

In the "Fear" chapter, we learned that we needed to change our thinking first in order to allow ourselves to take the actions needed to build confidence. Now we need to implement another strategy that will help us find some of the steps it's going to take.

PERSIST

The first thing we need to do once we have convinced ourselves that what we want is possible is to start talking about it. You will find mixed advice in this area (some with a scarcity mind-set will encourage you to keep your ideas secret), but I am a proponent of sharing your dream with the people around you and with those you meet.[4] I teach sharing your dream with people because this is how you train others to work on your behalf. What do I mean by this?

Every person inherently wants to be of service to others, and by telling them what you are passionate about, they can introduce information into the conversation that may help you. I can't tell you how many relationships I've built after having a conversation with someone and telling them about a goal that I had. It went something like, "I know someone who does that!" or "You know, I know someone you should get in contact with."

These types of leads won't come with every conversation, but in telling others what you are into and what you do, they will see you through the lens of your dream. By this I mean if you tell them you are a professional speaker and they hear a conversation about speakers, they will be reminded of you. They may even give your name as a reference!

If you hadn't told or spoken about your dream, that reference would not be connected to you, but because you stepped out on faith and spoke your vision into the world, you can reap the benefits of this simple action. Most think of action as physically doing something, but in some cases, the only action needed that pays off is simply opening your mouth to speak.

As you start to speak more about your dreams, you may come across opportunities to meet people who are living the life you want. I mentioned earlier about seeking out opportunities to increase your luck of being in the right place at the right time. All of this can be facilitated by sharing your dream every chance you get and following up with information that is given to you. This information can come in the form of potential conferences to attend or info on local meetings or identifying people in your circle who know other people in the field.[5]

The next thing you need to do is:

Find an Example (a Mentor)

A mentor is someone who is years ahead of you in his or her life progression, someone you look up to, who has some of the results you want. When I look for a mentor, I first look at results. These results aren't always business related. Many of them are lifestyle related as well. If I see someone who has an amazing marriage, I consider them for a potential marriage mentor. If I see someone who has a successful business, they may be a business mentor for me. The idea is to find people who have produced results and ask them to help you do it too.[6]

In my case of trying to become a doctor, there were several physicians I had met and shadowed who I could call and ask questions. Some of these connections came from my mother; others I sought out myself. These mentors would later write letters of recommendation for me and make phone calls on my behalf. The ability to call and talk to someone who was where I wanted to be was priceless. They would simply mention things in passing that were unknown to me. I would benefit from spending time and just having lunch with them.

Finding a mentor can be tough. After I was a physician and had the idea of writing a book, I had no authors in my network. As I began to tell people I was writing a book, like clockwork people started introducing me to other authors. These authors would be my initial sounding board for all my ideas. They clued me in on websites I didn't know about and resources that were available and gave me invaluable advice as I was starting out.

Not everyone will always be willing to help you, but that is okay. It takes time to develop a mentor/mentee relationship, so don't get discouraged if your first few choices don't work out. You will find the perfect match in due time; just keep searching.

One of the misconceptions of the mentor/mentee relationship is that the mentee doesn't have much to do in the relationship. This is far from the truth, and I'd even venture that the mentee is the glue that makes the relationship stay productive and cohesive. As a mentee, you should regularly update your mentor on your actions. You should follow up with him or her every few months and request in-person meetings. Mentors may have several other mentees they spend time with as well. It's your job to make sure you stay fresh in your mentor's mind by reaching out regularly. Updates are the best way; communication that is regular and doesn't have requests or questions attached every time is key to keeping the relationship healthy.

Success Leaves Clues

After you have broken the flawed logic that has kept you inactive, you can now start to talk it up. After you've ingrained talking about your dream every chance you get, it's now time to find that mentor. After you have found your mentor, it's study time. I suggest finding the mentor first, because he or she can weigh in on potential sources for study material.

You may be saying that you didn't sign up to go back to school. I understand that, but to be a master in your field, you've got to know your craft. This only comes with hours of studying the market and industry leaders who came before you. Success leaves lots of clues. You can simply study the actions of someone you admire, and in doing so, you will be obtaining his or her blueprint of what worked.[7] You will also become privy to things that didn't work for that person. Part of the reason we need to study is so we won't make the same mistakes. There is an old saying that history repeats itself, and it is certainly true. Part of this is because fewer and fewer people are willing to put in the study time to learn about those who came before them.

Next-Steps-*Only* Strategy

The last concept I want to introduce at this point is the idea of what I call the "next-steps-only" strategy. With this strategy, you only focus on the next step as you get started. Many of us are frozen with "paralysis by analysis" in the beginning as we try to map out the entire journey from where we are to where we want to be, steps A–Z.

The truth is, plans will change, and you will have to recalculate more times than you can imagine. Does this negate the fact that you need to have a formal direction and goal? No, but in order to create momentum in the beginning, it is sufficient to know only the next step.[8] We can all come up with what we can do next, what we can research next, who we can call next, and what we can freshen up on next.

The how-to guide may not have been created for your dream yet, but it only takes knowing the next step to get started.

Beat: *I Don't Know How*

Start: Researching a mentor and implementing the "next-steps-*only*" strategy

6

Timing

It's Not the Right Time.

Age is a case of mind over matter. If you don't
mind, it don't matter.
—Satchel Paige

I have often heard during conversations about dreams and goals that it just isn't the right time. This is a very common reason people tell themselves they shouldn't pursue their vision right now. It's the hurry-up-and-wait game that some of us play in our lives. Waiting for the right time or the perfect time is simply another form of procrastination. In my experience in working with clients to achieve greater things in their lives, I've found that this "perfect timing" doesn't really exist.[1]

It may work in other areas, like investing; people say you've got to buy low and sell high. There is also of a timing component to finding a good deal, but when it comes to creating our dreams, now is always the right time to be working toward it.

This timing discussion is very different from the time we talked about in chapter 4. In chapter 4, we were talking about finding time. In this discussion, it's about when to start. When is it time to bring the product to the market? When is it the right time to quit your job?

When is it the right time to have kids? When can I start to be the person I've always wanted to be?

We are always searching for the "right time," and we use our brainpower to try to make the best decision, but does it really make that big of a difference? I'm going to say no and stick to my no throughout this chapter. If you've found yourself saying that the timing isn't right, then when will it be the right time? Have you qualified what the right time is like? What are the criteria for the right time, and how detrimental would it be if you just did it now?

There is always a reason waiting to be used when rationalizing inaction. This is the easiest part to do. We can always tell ourselves a good story about playing it safe.[2] That's what most people do. I am challenging you to take action now. Get moving now. Stop waiting. Your time is now.

Too Young

The first time I told someone I wanted to become a professional speaker, he asked me what qualified me to be speaker. Initially, I had a very difficult time answering this question. I would always start to question myself when someone would challenge my authority to speak. Many people would ask what I had been through. What did I have to say at twenty-eight years of age? What would make someone want to listen to me? Ironically enough, it was never a speaker who asked me this. It was always someone who wasn't in the business.

One of the things you will find as you begin to think about timing is that there is always more that can be done. There are always more experiences to be had. There is always more practice time to line up. It's time for us all to get in the game and see what the league is about. It's time to get out there on the field and stop telling yourself you're not ready. Because you are ready; so what if you fall on your face the first time! The only thing that gets hurt is your ego, but we learn from each mistake and advance forward.

I finally started telling people it was my passion that qualified me. It was the burning desire to share my message that made me able to be a speaker. Most folks wouldn't challenge me on that one, but some would still ask what I would speak about. I would tell them I'm an expert in my life story. I was the best person to tell that story, so no one could take that expertise away from me. All that mattered was that I was driven enough to make it happen.[3]

My first speech was at a high school graduation, and believe it or not, the principal wanted me to speak so much that he never asked me how many other talks I had given! It ended up not being a factor at all, as I continued to book talks from referrals after my first one. I was now building that experience everyone was talking about, but if I hadn't stuck my neck out and just started to offer my services as a speaker, I never would have gotten my first gig.

I could have listened to the story I was getting from other people—the one that said I was too young to offer value as a speaker; the one that said I needed more experience to call myself a speaker; the one that said I needed to accomplish more so I could qualify myself as a speaker. I chose not to listen to any of those stories and just started to offer value to other people. As a result, I now have a speaking business where I speak regularly around the world.

Why the Stories Matter

I tell these stories from my life for a few reasons, the primary reason being to help you understand that these are some of the things you will have to persist through. If you are stuck waiting for the right time, this is an example where the right time was right then. My theory is that if you understand the psychology behind what is holding you back, you are able to make better and more intentional decisions about overcoming it.

I don't mention these stories to impress you, but to *impress upon you* the reality that some of the stories we tell ourselves simply aren't true. In theory, if you have counter evidence to the "truths" you tell yourself, you are more capable and willing to accept and apply other story options in your life.

These other stories could start with the idea that *so-and-so didn't wait to get started, so why should I?* They could start with the simple question, "Why not me; why not now?" There are tons of examples of young people starting companies, inventing things, going pro, or getting the big record deal. There are endless examples of people who didn't wait for the right time; they seized the moment and created the right time.

Be careful not to allow the "believing in luck" rationale to take away from these truths. Don't let the thought, "Well, they were just at the right place at the right time" be the reason you don't pay attention to the many examples before you. The bottom line is that many people traded being timid for taking action, and their results manifested because of those actions.

I'll continue to build my case of why perfect timing doesn't exist. Enter Colonel Sanders.

Too Old

Many of you may have heard this story already, but I'll give you the highlights here. After holding many jobs and starting a restaurant that grew in popularity, Colonel Harland Sanders decided at the age of sixty-two that he would expand his reach a bit. Well, expanding his reach is a gross understatement. At sixty-two, he decided he would take his fried chicken recipe and franchise the use of it across the United States.

In doing this, he created what is now known as KFC, one of the largest restaurant chains in the world, second only to McDonald's in 2015. How did a sixty-two-year-old man believe that at his age it was the *perfect time* for him to build the second-largest restaurant chain in the world? I would venture that he didn't consider his age. He just knew he had a vision and believed he could pull it off, so he went for it.

I have seen many individuals take themselves out of the running because they believe they are too old or that their time has passed. This doesn't have to be senior citizens either; I've heard "my time has passed" from twentysomethings concerning their dreams as well.

Why do we believe our dreams have an optimal timeline? Why do we place these stringent rules on ourselves about when we are capable of doing something? If Colonel Sanders can start a massive franchise empire in his sixties, you can pretty much do whatever you want at any age.

Part of persisting in this area is understanding that there are potentially multiple time periods that can work for you. In essence, there are multiple "right times." Having it laid out in your mind when you think things have to happen can only hinder you. Let go of the limited storyline, and give yourself some slack. Give yourself a chance to try again. It may not be the perfect storyline, but it's your storyline, so make it great.

If you feel like your time has passed and you are too old to do what you're put on earth to do, I've got one truth for you: you're still alive for that reason!

Someone Has Already Done It

Others may think that their dream isn't possible because someone took their idea or someone else has already done it. As I talk to people about their dreams, I never hear a shortage of good ideas. Many say, "Well, I had this idea, but then someone else did it before I did." Let's look into that logic for a minute.

In business, it is always useful to see if there is a potentially qualified buyer segment that will spend money on your offering. A company that is first to market can have a tough time identifying and qualifying their early-adopter buyer segment. The early adopters are the people who want the newest thing on the market and don't mind buying things that aren't tested in the market first. If you truly have an original idea and it's not simply improving a current product, you will need early adopters to be successful.

In the case of a second-to-market product, you have the benefit of watching the first to market trip and fall and figure things out *for you*. You will have your own challenges, but if you're not the first, you can benefit from the first company blazing the trail. Why am I talking about this when it comes to someone "taking your idea"? Let's look at a company many of us know well: Facebook.

Facebook was not the first to the social-media market; they were actually second to a website called MySpace. MySpace was almost exactly like Facebook, but you had many other features like more ability to customize what your profile looked like. If the founders of Facebook were of the mind-set that someone else had already done it, they would have stalled in building Facebook into what it is today. Instead they looked at what MySpace did, where they failed, where they stumbled, and so on. They studied what people were complaining about and made Facebook better. In their case, they benefited immensely by not being first.

That leads me to my next thought about being first, second, last, or whatever.

We may think that in the world there can only be one of anything or that there is limited space for only one best in a market. I remember when I was thinking about starting my company, I thought it had to be as big as Wal-Mart. I remember thinking I couldn't be a success until I was that big. Then I met a small-business owner and saw how he lived. His lifestyle was one I dreamed of, and he only worked in one state! This interaction completely changed the way I thought about business, influence, money, and success.

The truth is that there is room for many people to do well in this world. There is room for many of us to be the best. I first read this concept in a book by Dr. Jason Richardson, *It's All BS*. He wrote that you could be the best too, meaning there is room at the top for many bests.[4] After I thought about it for a bit, I started to test the idea and found evidence that this was, in fact, the truth.

If you think of anyone who is the best at something, there is a "class," if you will, that this person is a part of. That means when you consider who is the best, you think of many people who are the best in that moment. There are many companies that are the "best" at burgers. I think by most people's standards we can consider McDonald's, Burger King, Sonic, and In & Out successful. They are the best in the business of burger. The same is true for the best athletes in a sport. That is why we have the Hall of Fame, which is filled with the best.

Your timing is a small factor in your ability to be the best or one of the best in your field. What matters more than anything is your work ethic and drive to get yourself to the top. That is the most important factor in the equation. I've seen enough biographies to realize that someone will find benefits (timing being one of them) that you had while starting and will argue that was in your favor.[5] My argument is it's more about your point of view and what you believe at the time, not the timing itself.

I'll now dip over into some of the nuts and bolts about starting a new direction. These are things to consider once you have made your mind up that it's time for you to take action.

Timing in the Market for Entrepreneurs

Differentiation/Value Added

If you are looking to go into a new career, start a company, or are working on your initial plan of attack, you want to consider the differentiating factors you bring to the table. In any market, you will have competition, but differentiation is all about what is out there; it is also about your proposition to your customer. In the realm of getting a new job or starting a career, your customer can be seen as the hiring director. In the case of a new product or company, your customer is your ideal buyer. Believe it or not, we are always selling something when it comes to creating the life we dream of. Our ability to "sell" can make a lot of difference when it comes to our experience.

Differentiation can be thought of as your unique qualities. What makes you different? What makes you stand out? This is at the core of creating a great strategy, so spend some time thinking about the answers to those questions. Your ability to articulate these differentiating factors is going to be crucial during the "sales" process (interviewing, etc.). In business, potential investors, if you are pitching to venture capitalists (VCs), will want a business proposal. In the proposal, there is a section on market research and strategy. Your strategy will be based on your research of the market and your understanding of where you or your company fit in.

Will you enter the market and compete on price? Will you enter and compete as a premium option? Will you compete by adding value to what's already out there?

There are many ways for you to compete, and your understanding of the market, be it the job market or your specific sector, is critical. Again, this philosophy is adaptable to many models, and I only introduce the concept of differentiation to help you start to think about these types of things as you make your action plan to move forward.

In some cases, your differentiation will be that you are able to bring more value to the table. Value is something you possess that can help you, your employer, or your company reach its goals. Value can be anything, really—your experience, your talents, your gifts, etc. The key is to be able to look at what is being offered currently and delineating how you are adding more to that. The value added doesn't have to be unique in and of itself. You can articulate the value added in terms of "in addition to," or you can offer more of something, etc. The options of value creation are endless; it's really up to you to decide where you can best add value and how to communicate that value to your customer.

It Isn't Always an Either/Or

Situations aren't always black and white. Often we think of competition as solely an either/or option, meaning a customer, an employer, or a VC must make a choice on one option or the other. There may be times when both options are feasible. In other words, it isn't always A or B; it can also be AB. I bring this up in relation to timing because many think if there is something else out there and they haven't completely delineated their differentiation or value added, they have trouble seeing how they can enter a market.

The easy example I will use in this case is the music industry. Many consumers of music are fans of several artists. As such, they purchase Artist A's album, and they also purchase Artist B's album. You can liken this example to the concept of there being many bests in an industry.

Why is this important? As you consider when to take action, give yourself many ways to compete. In the end, you will only know once you have tried. If you aren't too old and you aren't too young, so what if someone else has already done it? You can be in addition too. There is always a place for you to pursue your vision. Believing in you means believing in your God-given talents; your purpose will create space for you in the world.

Beat: *It's Not the Right Time*

Start: Taking action now and solidifying your value proposition

7

Circumstances

My Circumstance Won't Allow It.

The last of human freedoms—the ability to choose
one's attitude in a given set of circumstances. —
Viktor E. Frankl

Initially, adverse situations or circumstances we find ourselves in can seem to have significant power over our life's trajectory. In this chapter, I focus on circumstance as one of the reasons people quit on their dreams. We all have had a moment when something just didn't quite go our way. We may have found ourselves in a position where we felt we didn't have much power.

Circumstances can include many situations or positions in life, but in this chapter I'll focus on the aspects of life a person is likely to think he or she didn't have anything to do with—things like where you were born, your family, your athletic ability, your natural talents, etc. These situations have the unique ability to be severely disempowering (if viewed negatively) because they are "out of our hands."

Viktor Frankl

Viktor Frankl found himself in a very rough situation for a significant period of his life. He was one of the many Jews who were taken captive and placed in concentration camps during the Holocaust. He discusses his experiences and thought processes in the classic book *A Man's Search for Meaning*. I want to share a bit of his story here, because he found himself in a very disempowering position, but despite his situation, he was able to empower himself in the moment through his focus and perspective.

After being taken prisoner and seeing many of your family killed, one can only imagine what there was to hold on to. Frankl talks specifically about the mind-set of the prisoners and how their focus determined their outcomes in many cases. He was one of the few who survived the Holocaust and lived to teach about it later in life. But what helped him get through this experience in a manner where he actually found power while being held captive?

Frankl talks about controlling his thoughts and his sense of hope while being exposed to horrific treatment. His ability to maintain hope in the future was critical to how he conducted himself while in the concentration camps. This idea of a better day or a reunion with his family was a piece of his mental strategy to stay focused. He also focused on maintaining as much of his personal dignity as he could, considering the circumstances. He saw others giving up in their minds, and as a result, it was obvious when you noticed how they took care of themselves. It was also clear who had given up when you looked at how they treated others in the camp.

Frankl was able to look at the situation and focus on the areas of his life that he did have control over. With so many things out of his control, he realized that even though his captors may have had control over his external environment, he had control of his internal environment.[1] He had control of the thoughts that he dwelled on. He had the power to focus his energy and brainpower toward things that were positive, instead of ruminating over the aspects of his current situation he had no control over.

As a result of his amazing ability to maintain a positive mind-set, Frankl arrived on the other side victorious. He lived to tell his story, and because of it, I was blessed to gain better perspective in my life.

One thing that has been shown to be true throughout history is that individuals who face adversity early in life are better equipped in many cases to handle adversity later in life.[2] In the case of entrepreneurs, one example is in the case of dyslexic children.

A reading disability caused by a deficit in the phonologic component of language, dyslexia is found to be common among many ultra-successful entrepreneurs—Richard Branson, Charles Schwab, and Damon John, to name a few.[3] Intuitively, this may not make sense. If you have a reading disability in our society, this can easily present quite an array of challenges for you. From social issues to learning and advancing in school, living with dyslexia can be extremely challenging for children. The typical diagnosis is made before the age of ten.

This disability, however, led them to develop in other areas of their lives, to compensate for what they lacked in reading ability. These skills can include things like relationship building, delegation, emotional intelligence, and communication skills. Dyslexics had to lean on these areas more at an early age and as a result developed them on a deeper level.

In business, persistence, relationship building, and communication can be great advantages to have when making deals or leading a team. In this light, you wouldn't question dyslexics running some of the largest companies today. It would actually make sense. Malcolm Gladwell addressed this issue in his book *David and Goliath* as he retold the greatest underdog stories of all time.[4]

Circumstances don't always have to be the end of the story. We always have the ability to change our minds and decide to give it a different meaning. We can decide to play our hand a different way. We can decide that another outcome is possible for us. The thing with circumstances is that they have the ability to make people think there is no way out. They are taken in a matter-of-fact way and not challenged in our brains. Many of the circumstances we find ourselves in may not be completely our fault. Someone else may have had a hand in our circumstance, but that isn't a reason to believe you can't now change things.

In all actuality, as in the case of Viktor Frankl, you may not physically be able to change the circumstance or situation, but you can change the way you see it. What really needs to change is your thought process around the limitations that accompany your circumstances.

I remember when I was younger, with just my mom and sister at home with me, my mother had to work three jobs at times to make enough money for ends to meet. My mother, no matter what, always continued to believe there was a better day coming for us. She worked and worked and eventually built not one but two homes later in life. In watching her look at circumstances as temporary setbacks, I learned that nothing was final. All things on the table could be changed; it was all up to the way I thought about the situation.[5]

Compromise

One thing that becomes a result of unforeseen circumstance is compromise. We find ourselves in a situation and figure the only way to move forward is to make some sort of compromise to endure. In the case of having a family, many will believe that there is no room to pursue their dreams because they have to provide a steady income for their family. The compromise may look like the responsible thing to do in the beginning, but with a small compromise here and a few more there, we may find ourselves far away from our vision for our lives.

PERSIST

I look at it this way: if you are ever planning on telling your kids to live their dreams, or if you are planning to tell them that they can do anything they put their minds to, *you* must be the first example of that. Your story will be more believable if your child is not only hearing that from his or her parent but is also watching the parents living their dreams daily. This is a much more powerful position than the "do as I say" motivation option.

What will your story be when your kids ask you what your dreams were? Will you have a story for your child at that point? Will you have a reason why things didn't work out for you? You can't say to them it was because you started having kids. What, now *they* are the reason you aren't living your dreams? We must do better for ourselves and for our children. A great goal would be to never have your children ask you what your dream was. They will already know the answer to this because they watch you live it every day.

Compromise is warranted in some settings, and many of us will have to make sacrifices to live our vision, but the vision must continue. We cannot, in our attempts to adjust for a circumstance, put our dreams on the shelf. We aren't called to live a life where we continuously adjust to our circumstance. Living day to day, putting out fire after fire with no direction, is not much of a life at all. To build an amazing life, we must maintain a quest that has a destination and a direction every day.[6]

One of our greatest advantages as humans is the ability to focus on one thing, but in doing so, we have an even greater ability to ignore stimuli that aren't relevant to our goals. I am not saying we should ignore situations in our lives; I'm saying we can choose not to dwell on the negative and shift our focus and energy toward what is going to help us get what we want.

This ability plays out every day we leave our homes. A simple walk down the street can be the perfect example. As you walk, there may be hundreds of conversations going on around you, but you ignore them. You recognize they are there, but you focus on sounds and conversations that are relevant to you. Maybe you are walking with a friend and are tuned in to her voice. Maybe you're waiting for the stoplight to change colors and are zoned in on the light on the other side of the intersection. Maybe you're walking near a construction site and are looking around to avoid running into something that is normally not there.

There are many opportunities for us to concentrate on the wrong things if we do not have an overall focus driving us. Why am I talking about focusing while walking down the street? This is a very simple example of someone on a mission with the ability to ignore or tune out things that are not relevant in the moment. There will always be a distraction waiting to turn you away from your vision, and in many of our lives, circumstances do just that.

We start to look at the circumstance and everything that comes with it more than we focus on the direction we'd like to take our lives. To stay with the walking example, this leads to being distracted by the construction site and turning around and walking home. We see our normal path is blocked and that we can't move or stop the construction, so we figure there is no way to continue. We'll have to compromise and wait for the circumstances to change.

This is a very simple and unlikely example, but I use it to emphasize the point. We get distracted from the main goal and don't use our brainpower to consider ways to get around the construction. Every obstacle can be overcome, but formulating that plan is based on where your brainpower is being used. Now, the game has become a game of allocating brainpower.

Where is most of your critical thinking spent? Is it spent thinking about the limitations that come along with your circumstance, or is spent exploring ways to circumvent your situation? These are very basic questions, and I think most would agree that you are going to see results in the areas where you spend the most brainpower.

It is now time for you to explore critically where your brainpower is spent. If you are hoping to find ways to overcome your circumstance, spend more critical-thinking time on it. Ignore the urge to fixate on the obstacles, instead focus on figuring out how to beat them.

I Had No Choice

Have you ever heard people say that they didn't have a choice? In most cases, we do have a choice, assuming we didn't just break the law and are on our way to jail! Our acknowledgment of this choice is where the real issue lies. Are we bold enough to acknowledge that we always have a say in the direction of our lives? When we say we don't have a choice, in a way we are taking the responsibility out of our hands and placing it on who- or whatever gave you the choice. This is a passive position and one that projects the responsibility externally.

One of the best decisions I ever made in my life was when I decided, no matter what happened to me, that I would take 100 percent responsibility for the results. No matter what, good or bad, I would take the responsibility. When I made this choice, I started to intentionally exert my influence in every situation. I no longer would accept the status quo or "that's just the way it is" as an answer for my life. In that moment, I took control of my life and decided if I created the results, that also empowered me to change those results.

Even though, at times, we may feel that we don't have a choice, we must use our brainpower and focus to figure out how we can influence the situation. This is where our time is best spent. Instead of believing that all the choices have been made for us, we must insert our personal choice into every situation to ensure we can persist in pursuing our dream, despite a setback.

I talk about circumstances that can potentially negatively affect our lives, because these are the ones that people usually have the toughest time dealing with. In moments when we feel something is going in our favor, we never complain. We simply consider the new options that are on the table and make the best decision for ourselves at that time. We must share the same attitude if it is something that initially seems to be unfavorable. We must look at the options that are on the table and move forward. "I have no choice" places us again in an inactive state. The excuses that we tell ourselves work to keep us from taking action. Now, there is one last thing to consider. Are all setbacks truly unfavorable?

The Favorable Setback

"There are no mistakes in life, only lessons."
—Robin Sharma

Instead of looking at a circumstance or situation as a setback or something to blame, there is a school of thought that endorses all adversity as favorable. What can that mean? Failing that test or being abused as a child is a good thing? I think there are limits to every mantra, but my point here is to recognize when something has become a limiting story in our lives. If you haven't drawn from a tough experience any lessons learned or advantages from the struggle, it is quite possible you are caught in a cycle of blame or excuse.

On the subject of finding our purpose, many of us have pain that is the exact fuel that drives us forward to righting a wrong or correcting something in the world that needs improving. In the light, an adversity (the cause of the pain) is now used to drive you forward. You can look at it as if you now have an additional gear of motivation to tap into when you're running low on drive.

Having a mind-set that values finding growth in as many situations as possible is exactly what we need to overcome circumstance.[7] If we are looking for a lesson or an area of growth when it comes to struggle, we can change the meaning of the struggle. We can move the circumstance into something that gives us strength or a lesson we now value and teach to others. We can find use for the story, instead of allowing it to disempower us and keep us in inaction. I'll talk more about failure in the next chapter.

So, how do we persist through circumstance?

As we learned through the story of Viktor Frankl, we can choose to focus on the areas in our lives where we do have control. By taking control of the areas we can influence, we insert more intention into our lives. This counters the thought that things are totally out of our control. With this strategy, we work to find areas we can improve about our lives, even as we are going through a tough situation. We persist in moving forward by asserting our influence in the smallest areas. This can turn a disabling situation into something that can't completely stop us. As we start with the small areas, we can work to take back total control of our lives. In the case of Frankl, we can survive the unthinkable and live to teach others about it.

In the case of dyslexics, we learned that an unfavorable situation (on the surface) can actually lead to advancement in other areas of life. This can potentially lead to talent in areas of life that others haven't spent as much time cultivating. So, the ability to persist can also be based in your ability to see the silver lining in the circumstance. This silver lining may not be visible to others, but it's your focus that is in question. If you are able to find a silver lining in your situation, you can displace its power to keep you stuck in inaction and move through it.

If a past circumstance is keeping you stuck, persisting in spite of it is all about creating a compelling picture for the future. Are you focusing on the setbacks that come with the circumstance, or are you looking past them? This, like the case of choosing to focus on what you control, is about choosing to take your focus back, away from the setbacks surrounding circumstance. To persist, we must believe we have a chance, and after changing our focus to possibilities, we are now able to continue to move forward.

Once you have freed your focus from the nonproductive, you have time and brain space to think about what you can do to help move your agenda forward. There is always room for you to flex more. By *flex* I mean make adjustments, try something new, use another strategy, etc. Flexing is about seeing where you have wiggle room and taking advantage. Taking advantage leads to more intentional actions surrounding your dream.

Lastly, if you find yourself in a circumstance where you feel like you don't have a choice, you first need to ask yourself a few questions.

Why do I believe I have no choice?

What do I have a say in?

Is this no-choice mentality a copout?

Once we have come to grips with our positions around these questions, we are now able to move forward and persist through it. In most cases, believing you don't have a choice is one of the easier ways to explain a less-than-ideal situation. It takes a stronger and more responsible position to acknowledge where you did play a role in a given situation. In order to persist, you must move this "I have no choice" position out of your way first. Believing this takes all of the power away from you, and when we believe we don't have power, we are more likely not to act.

Don't let circumstance be the end of the story for you; make an intentional decision to remove limiting beliefs about your situation and replace them with what remains possible. Broaden your horizon and increase what you are certain is possible.

Beat: *My Circumstance Won't Allow It*

Start: Focusing on opportunities instead of obstacles.

8

Failure

I've Tried and Failed.

Never confuse a single defeat with a final defeat.
—F. Scott Fitzgerald

We have now circled back to a discussion I started in chapter 1 on fear. In chapter 1, we talked mostly about the fear of failure. This fear is what keeps us from attempting a new challenge. On the timeline, this type of fear kicks in to try to keep you from ever failing in the first place. Put another way, this type of fear keeps you from getting started.

What we will talk about in this chapter is actual failure, times when you tried something and it didn't work out; times when you took the test and didn't ace it; times when you fell flat on your face. We are now talking about the sting that comes from underperformance in the eyes of others and in your mind.

Failure has stopped folks from trying again for many reason. If we overemphasize the result (failure), we can overshadow the analysis of our strategy and methods. When we see this failure as the be-all and end-all or we take the matter-of-fact position, we back ourselves into a corner that is tough to get out of. This corner can tell us that's just the way it is. It can tell us that *we* are the failure. It can tell us that we will *always* get the same result.[1]

When we fail, there are several fundamental questions we must ask ourselves before we come to a conclusion about what it really means to us. First, we must decide what it says about us. Is this about me personally, or is it about something or someone else?

Secondly, we must decide on our ability to produce different results. Can I get any better? How much can I realistically improve?

Then, we must decide our position on future attempts. Should we even try again? Can we likely change the outcome?

When we choose disempowering positions to these questions, we run the risk of convincing ourselves never to try again, or we convince ourselves to smaller risks in the future and never truly reach our fullest potential. Our beliefs when it comes to failure have a massive effect on our ability to persist afterward. In order to learn how to persist after failure, we must take some time and truly consider our thought process after a failure.

I'm a Failure

If, after failure, your resulting thought is that *you* are a failure, you've now taken one occurrence and turned it into your life. Failure is just one event; it is not a person—but many of us at times are tempted to come to this conclusion. It is one of the easier positions to take, since it takes major courage to get up and try again after you have failed. You can sit and pout for a while and say to yourself "I'm the failure," but it takes guts to get back up and go for it again. Don't let "I am a failure" be your copout. Don't let this thought be the reason you don't try something else. Your result, whatever it may be, is more a reflection of your strategy than it is a reflection of you. As for your strategy, well, you can change that!

We can go even deeper and talk about the fact that you came up with the failing strategy, so maybe all your strategies will fail. There are many alternatives to this, and I will offer a few here. You don't have to come up with the strategy; you can hire someone for that. Maybe you just try another strategy and give yourself some slack. No one is perfect; if you've failed at something, that means you're just like everyone else.

We must work to separate ourselves from the failure and look at the situation as objectively as possible. Becoming self-aware and fine-tuning your ability to look at yourself critically is a major key to success. Those who are able to look at themselves for areas of improvement are best suited to compete in the world. This, however, takes great courage, and it also takes humility. For you to look at yourself for areas of improvement, you must first understand that you are not perfect. Pride and ego will mislead you into thinking you are infallible, but this is a lie.

Also, as you fail, you must understand that it is not a true and complete reflection of you. You are more than a business model or a grade on a test or a partner in a relationship. The totality of you is more than a single occurrence. You are more than your failures. Persisting through this builds the very important virtue of patience.[2]

I'll Never Be or Get Good Enough

This thought or conclusion leads us to quit our preparation. This is working to stop you before you get started. It is interesting that many fail to try again because they have convinced themselves that it isn't worth the effort. This keeps many people away from their dreams. It isn't how hard something is, it is how convinced a person is about the odds of achieving it. We must believe that our hard work will pay off. We must believe we are capable of playing at our best and that preparation is going to get our performance closer to that personal best. We have to believe in the work that will get us there.

If you tell yourself you'll never get good enough, why try?

After failure and even after trying your best, you can improve. As long as you have time on this earth, (i.e., you're still breathing), you can improve. Today's mastery is the result of yesterday's work. So, if you continue to work, you can continue to improve that mastery level.

The more you power through thoughts that you can't get good enough, the more fuel you'll have to power through future failures.[3] One of the best illustrations I know to explain this I got from my training in surgery. One of my first mentors was a general surgeon, and one of the common things surgeons say is that if you aren't prepared to handle the complications of a procedure, you aren't ready to do that procedure.

This is profound on many levels, but on the surface, this statement implies that you are going to have complications. If you thought you were the best surgeon in the world and that you were incapable of failure, why would you need to understand how to handle complications? You'd do every procedure perfectly, right? If you were to pick a surgeon to operate on you, wouldn't you want the one who could handle complications? If you do want the one who can handle complications, you'd want the one with experience with something not going right.

Hmmm, isn't that interesting?

We'd want the surgeon who has experienced a complication, but we expect perfection from ourselves? I hope you get my point. Complications, failures, and missteps are all things that help us improve. They make us better.

Lessons Are Found in Failure

As we endure failure, we reap the benefits of its pain. If we keep the mind of a student, instead of focusing on our mishaps, we look for lessons. That is the beauty of failure: it teaches you what doesn't work.[4] As we look for solutions, knowing what doesn't work is just as important as knowing what does. As children, we learn constantly, but we are called children and understand that we are children. This keeps us in a mind-set of learning. When we become adults, some of us lose that focus and believe we are no longer supposed to learn daily.

Keeping the mind-set of a child is critical to seeing the value in failure. As I said before, we must look at failure as objectively as possible. Look for the lesson. Ask questions: What can I learn from this? How can I use this knowledge? How am I better because this happened?

One of my favorite subjects in high school and college was math. I really loved working problems and seeing the numbers on the page, erasing and correcting my work. There were many times in high school when I left the table crying because I couldn't figure out a homework question. My math homework would take my total focus, and I loved the reward of getting a right answer. Why am I mentioning my love for math and my tendency to make numerous mistakes?

When I was a medical student, I worked tutoring nursing students in medical mathematics. I realized really quickly that I was great at tutoring, because most of the problems the students had with capturing the material I had had myself. In almost every session, my student would work through a problem and make a mistake that I had made years earlier when I was learning the same material.

In each occasion, I would remember why I initially thought that was the way to the correct answer. One of the things that helped me build rapport with my students was my ability to explain back to them how

I had thought the same thing initially. As I walked them through their mistake and explained the logic, I was able to capture their attention and guide them to the proper strategy.

The most important aspect of this story is that I made the mistakes too. I learned and became better because I worked through my mistakes.[5] Now, the fact that I made so many mistakes helped me explain and teach others. This leads me to the next advantage of failure: you grow.

Growth through Failure

The easiest way I can explain this is through physiology. In college, I became obsessed with working out and growing muscle. I wanted to be "buff," as we called it back in the day. I looked at the guys who had the muscles and wondered how I could get the same results.

Muscle grows through a process called hypertrophy. The muscle cells actually grow in size as they are exposed to increased loads that typically accompany weight training. If anyone has worked out in the gym, you know sometimes there is pain involved. Usually after a hard set, your muscle is slightly oxygen deprived when you "feel the burn."

There is a type of repetition training that's called *training to failure* in working out. It's when you use a small amount of weight and you do repetitions until you can no longer do any more. You push the weight until failure. You push yourself to the limit, until you absolutely cannot push out one more rep.

The interesting thing about training to failure is the mentality that comes with it. There is still debate on what exact factors of training to failure help you the most, but we won't get into exercise physiology research with this one. How you think about failure is what I'm talking about and the growth that happens when you no longer fear failure.

The muscle growth that happens when you train to failure is a result of looking at failure as something to push through, something that is in your way of your next big goal. When I train in the gym, I'm looking to maintain strength and grow muscle. Looking toward failure and pushing through it allows me to get to the next set on the next day and no longer fear the failure that I faced the day before in the gym.

Not only does your muscle grow, your mind grows as well.[6] Your vision also grows. When you take on failure and overcome it, you start looking for greater challenges the next day. You push the weight up, and the next time around, you go to a higher level.

Ability to Relate (Impress or Impact) Sharing Failures

I'm shifting gears here to discuss a higher level of motivation. This is how you can use your failures to relate to others and lift them up. I alluded to this in my tutoring story, but I'll elaborate here. One of the things that isn't truly understood by most is that many times our failure and struggle isn't really about us. What could that mean? Why would we suffer for others? Why would we fail for others?

As I've grown, I've learned to thank God for my struggles. I thank Him for them for many reasons, but the lessons I learned, the growth that occurred. and the mental fortitude that resulted are worth gratitude themselves. Truly, why am I happy I struggled?

My reason for existence is to encourage others to see the power God has placed inside of them. This power must be acknowledged and internalized before you can really take determined action toward your vision and destiny. I believe the world is suffering when any person doesn't live his or her purpose.

Contrary to common perception, my greatest attributes are my failures. My failures have allowed me to relate to others in their moments of failure. They have allowed me, as I mentioned in my tutoring story, to build rapport with people. Failure breaks down barriers of impressiveness and allows me to be real and relatable. The moment someone says to me, "You're just like me," that's the moment I have succeeded. You need to understand that at the core, you have enough power to influence any area of your life. You have the ability to create your vision and actualize it, despite failure.

The understanding that failure is coming and that it's not as big a deal as you may think is key. With this understanding, there is no longer anything to fear, only failures to find and success to achieve.

One of my mentors was a retired US Air Force colonel, and as he talked to me about leadership and influence, one of the things I took with me was the notion of impact or impress. He told me that if I wanted to impress people, I should tell them about my successes. He told me to shower them with all the things I had accomplished. "Let them know how great you are." Then he said, "But if you want to impact them, if you want to change their life, tell them about your failures."

Your ability to impact others on the deepest level is rooted in how impressed they are with you. The more you strive to impress them, the less likely you are to impact them long term. Break down the barriers of impressiveness by being open about your failures. This makes you just like everyone else (which is the truth, but sometimes not believable) and able to gain their ear in conversation.

Desperation and the Energy that Comes with It

There is something to be said about the desperation that comes with failure and defeat. On one hand, you can ask who would want to welcome that into their lives. In my experience, when you really want something and things aren't going your way, desperation can set in.

PERSIST

Desperation isn't necessarily a complete loss; there is a certain energy that comes with desperation, and this energy can be harnessed.

When you're facing failure, you must do all you can to find energy and continue to move forward. If you don't want something so badly that you become desperate, well, you may not want it badly enough.

Your ability to stay gritty during tough times is one of the key indicators of your ability to succeed.[7] Persisting despite obstacles is a muscle that can be built through practice. Use these tools to increase your grit, and there won't be an obstacle that can stop you.

Beat: *I've Tried and Failed*

Start: Changing your strategy to change your results and never quit

9

Motivation

I can't stay motivated.

Of course motivation is not permanent. But then, neither is bathing; but it is something you should do on a regular basis.
—Zig Ziglar

Have you ever had what seemed to be a great idea and started working on it, only to run out of gas a few days, weeks, or months later? I'd argue that most people can relate to this situation.

Why is this? Why is it that we all have great ideas but run out of gas as we move toward actualizing them? I'm going to explore some of the top reasons folks say keep them from staying motivated. Then we'll discuss some ways you can counter this in your life.

Motivation is a fleeting feeling at times. It'd be great if we stayed on cloud nine at all times, but it doesn't really work that way. I could dedicate an entire book to the topic of why motivation fades, but here are a few of the reasons.

Lack of Periodic Reflection

When we first start to work on a project, many of us want to jump right into it. We get inspired to draw something and pull out the pencil to sketch it out immediately. We've been taught to keep the pen and pad next to our bed to scribble down great ideas that pop into our heads. Many of us are really great at capturing our ideas, but how or why we came up with that idea isn't always captured.

In a hurry, we start the work and ride the wave for a few days, maybe weeks—but then what? Do we wait for the next round of motivation that inspires us to take more action? This can potentially have you waiting for years. In today's society of fifteen minutes of fame, ADD, ADHD, and constant distraction, how are we to stay focused on one thing? How are we to realize what is a distraction and what is "the next big idea"?

First off, if it's motivation you seek, you must disconnect motivation from a feeling. It isn't the feeling that you should seek, because feelings will change over time. The best strategy I've discovered is crystallizing *why* we are doing something. Fully understanding this can act as fuel in times when you don't necessarily feel like doing work.[1]

One way to avoid these stalls in productivity is to schedule time to reflect on the reason you started. There will be times when the work may seem insurmountable or the barriers to entry into a market seem too high. This can seduce us into focusing on obstacles, which can drain our motivation.[2]

By scheduling regular times to reflect on the reason we started in the first place, we allow for time to reenergize after we've been in battle, trying to create our dreams. Reflection is a set-aside time to go back to the basics. Consider a few questions such as:

- Why is this so important?
- Why do you want to do this?
- Whom are you serving?
- To whom does this matter?

I've learned to enjoy reflection for several reasons; one of the most important is that it pushes me forward and gives me the nudge I need when I want to quit.

Surprising as it may be, we can forget why we started. It's an easy thing to do, once you are entrenched in the day-to-day operations of a venture. We can miss the forest by focusing on the trees.

Reflection also calls into question your actions in this moment, challenging you to connect today's busyness to the big picture or overall goal or strategy you started in the beginning. For some, the busyness can easily take over your entire calendar. Being busy is one of the easiest ways to trick yourself into thinking you're getting the important things done. Reflection allows time for you to analyze where you're spending your time and to test if these actives are critical.[3]

In reflection, we can see times when we have gotten off track or times when we have let a distraction steal our focus. By reflecting periodically, you can help prevent this sort of drifting. I recommend this be done weekly. Take time with your team or your accountability partner to discuss your motives and how this week or next week's activities connect to that.

One activity that can help facilitate reflection is journaling. Putting down your thoughts as you go through something can be very valuable to you in the future. You will have a mass of information you can reference to see where you've grown. You will also have the ability to tap into that original inspiration that sparked you beginning this journey. Lastly, this is a perfect time to celebrate your past success!

Many folks lose motivation because they have forgotten the basics about why they started. Strategic reflection can help you tap into that original drive.

Lack of Discipline

Discipline is a topic that many people downplay when they talk about motivation. Many times, it isn't the talented who prosper; it's the individuals who are most disciplined. I remember in college, as I was improving as a basketball player, I could see a direct correlation between my performance in the game and my workout schedule that week. The more focused or dedicated I was to the workouts during the week, the better I performed in the game.

Since we know motivation isn't just a feeling, we know that consistency is one of the things that help get us results. In this chapter, we're talking about ways to stay motivated, so stay with me as I get into the topic of discipline.

Many people may be saying, isn't this entire book about discipline, about persisting? Yes and no. Persisting involves discipline, of course, but as you may know, understanding mind-set and the stories we tell ourselves plays a huge role as well in our ability to keep going.

From nearly a decade as a military officer, I've learned a thing or two about discipline.[5] Discipline can be looked at simply as the story you tell yourself about why you should keep going. We may not always feel like continuing in a specific activity, but our discipline then takes over and reminds us why we are doing this. One of the things I remind people of often is this: even the work you do when you don't feel like it pays off.

When we first start to examine discipline, we must tear down our aversion to it. Many of us have told ourselves stories about discipline, and most of them aren't great! Who wants to be regimented? Who wants to be inflexible? These two words don't make people very excited, do they? Yet it is in discipline that we give ourselves the best chance of achieving our goal. So our success, in a way, is based in our discipline to do the necessary work.[6] If discipline hasn't been your strength up to this point, I have some suggestions that might help.

Numerous studies have shown that discipline is a major component of the ultra-successful.[4] People who are unable to stay on task are less likely to make it through tough times. Work ethic and discipline are about making a plan and seeing it through to completion.

If everyone has the ability to improve, why isn't everyone improving? The reason is simple: not everyone is dedicated to improving; we like the idea of it, but we aren't dedicated to the work needed to bring it about.

This is sometimes based on lacking the belief that you are personally able to improve or lacking the belief that the work will actually pay off. Many times, we can talk ourselves out of discipline because we convince ourselves the work isn't worth it. I think this is a great time to talk about beliefs.

Lack of Belief

The ones who believe they can improve are motivated to do the work to improve.

Motivation can lag when you aren't able to see the fruits of your hard work. Believing that the work actually makes the goal attainable is one of the foundations of motivation. We must believe first that we are capable of benefitting from our work.

You may want to make the results of others about the person. Many think it is the *person* who got the results. This is in stark contrast to believing the results came from a training regimen or effort. You see, it's really *not* about the person.

The results you admire are about the time that was put in; it's about the discipline, the strategy. That same strategy can be transported from person to person, and so can the results. So, as we are discussing ways to stay motivated, we are now breaking it down even further. You must believe your actions will pay off.

By working on your beliefs, it becomes easier to motivate yourself to take action. Let's go even further into this belief paradigm.

Motivation Is Based in Expectation

Let's turn beliefs into expectations. What does this mean? It means that not only do you believe your hard work will pay off, but you are *expecting* it to! Now, some may say this is impractical, but I'll use a simple example from basketball.

Why shoot a shot you aren't expecting to make? Yes, we take the shot because we *believe* we can make it. I'd argue that expectations are the highest determiner of your results. Those who actually expect to make the shots make more of them. I remember when I was playing in college, my shooting percentage went up and down with my confidence level. When I expected to make more shots, simply put, I did. In actuality, all I did was merely *changed my thoughts* about what I expected.

As you move to expectation, there will be very little lack of motivation. Why wouldn't you be motivated if you expected your action to breed the exact results you want? You see, it's not about *if*, when you're operating in expectation, you think only about *when*.

Not Focusing on Strengths

Motivation can also be drained when we spend too much time working on what we perceive as a weakness. I use the word *perceive* because it is all about the stories we tell ourselves. If you think something is a weakness in your life, don't spend too much time there. If you want to make it or transform it into a strength, you'll first need to change the story you tell yourself.

I'm talking about areas of your life that you have determined to be weaknesses. If you've made that determination, then don't spend too much time in that activity. Instead focus on your strengths and gifts. By spending too much time working on our weakness, we risk the chance of becoming discouraged too early in the process of improvement. You can also look at it like this: If you don't currently have that skill, is it worth the time developing it? Can you hire someone to do it for you?

We have all been given gifts by God, and most of us know what we're good at. We have an advantage when we are working in our strengths. It's a lot easier to get motivated to do something that you do very well.

When we have personally determined something to be a strength, we naturally have more confidence in that area. When you believe you have a strength, you are more likely to believe you can get results working in your area of strength. Do what you do well, and if there is some aspect of the process that you do not enjoy, I would encourage you to bring someone on your team who has that area as a strength. We all have a sweet spot and enjoy being in that space. You can promote that for others by seeking strengths in others that you haven't personally developed in yourself.

Lack of Service

One of the things I have found through my research and my personal life is that when you dedicate yourself to the service of others, it is easier to find motivation in low moments. We all will do more for others than we will do for ourselves on many occasions. As you move toward living out more of your purpose, you will find that you are intended to serve someone with your life. This also speaks to the idea of reflection and the practice of it; you can use it to remind you of whom you are serving.

Knowing that we are meant to serve others can help us to find and visualize that person every day. We can also work to crystallize who that person is when we have service in the forefront of our minds.

PERSIST

As we think about service as the backbone of our existence, we can align our gifts and identify who would benefit most from them.

The first few years of medical school were extremely tough for me. There were several reasons for this, but mostly I had never dedicated myself so much in my life. The discipline that was needed to get through was at a level I had never experienced before.

Needless to say, there were several moments when I wanted to quit. I remember one night specifically when I was tired and didn't want to study anymore. I thought about how tired I was and how great my body would feel if I allowed it to sleep. I also knew I would be behind on my reading schedule if I didn't finish the work for the day.

In that moment, I thought about my daughter and how I was working to create a better life for her and for my family. I visualized her face; I thought about how it would feel to be a great provider for her and the lifestyle I could create for us.

As I focused on who I was working for or serving, I felt infused with a new dose of motivation. I felt that my sleepiness was no match for my purpose, no match for my *why*. Serving my family was more important than sleep in that moment.

There will be moments when you won't feel motivated to keep going. In those moments, it's time to reflect about why you started, double down on your discipline, revisit your belief system, and identify whom you're serving. These are the strategies that will help you stay motivated when the road gets tough.

Beat: *I can't stay motivated*

Start: Frequent reflection on your "why" and a commitment to discipline and service

10

Comfort

I'm Comfortable.

Comfort can be our greatest enemy at times, but it seems many people are spending the majority of their lives in pursuit of comfort. Why am I going after comfort in this chapter, the very thing many of us tell ourselves we are seeking?

One of the things that is counterintuitive about living your dreams is that it will require you to leave your comfort zone. It will require you to take risks that are uncomfortable, to say the least. Comfort, this lukewarm place of coziness, can sometimes sing a lullaby to us that puts us right to sleep. It can lull our vision, and it can make us fearful of the unknown.

To some, this comfortable life that you have created is the very thing that is holding you back from pursuing your next vision. The fact that things are easier now is the very reason you don't go after something that is hard. It's the same reason you don't jump out of a cozy bed in the winter: you know it's going to be cold when you leave the covers!

I found myself in this very position as I contemplated leaving medicine full time. I had a comfortable job, paying me a comfortable salary, a reasonable work schedule, and a great place to live. Everything was comfortable—which was the problem.

I knew deep inside that I was meant to do other things. I had realized this even before I finished medical school. The writing had been on the wall for years, but it all was coming to the forefront. I realized if I didn't spend more time doing what I loved, I was going to let this job steal my life away. I was spending most of my time at the office, seeing patients, writing notes, and commuting in the car. I loved seeing patients and liked the one-on-one interaction I got to experience in the exam room, but something was missing.

Somehow, the interactions in the exam room were too superficial, I wanted to go deeper with my patients. I wanted to help change their lives, not just help cure their ailments with the latest treatment regimen science could offer. It was in these times that I felt the tug on my heart. It was time to move on.

But I was living a good life! I had a comfortable existence. I had everything I needed. I didn't really want for anything. My family was in a good neighborhood. What more could I ask for?

The very life I had once aspired to live and create was now holding me back from living my true destiny. I didn't want to lose all of the "things." I didn't want to recreate my life and income all over again. What was I thinking? I was comfortable, right?

What I realized was that all of the comfort I was living with was just a facade. I was just the story I told myself, and this led me to my next point: I was comfortable because I thought I was secure.

Security

Many of us are searching for security in life, and for most, that can come in the form of employment. I can't tell you how many times I have talked to folks about how their job is limiting their life. They tell me about things they want to do and then explain why they can't because they'll lose their job, and their job is their livelihood. In America, working is how we spend the majority of our time, but is this job really secure, or is that just what we are telling ourselves? Is there a way that you can be fired? Is that a possibility? Are you in an employment contract that says you can't be terminated?

As I looked at all of these questions in my life, I realized my life was no more secure than it was before I finished school. I could lose my job at any moment, no matter how unlikely I was told it was. No matter how well positioned I was in the job market, the business could let me go. So this security wasn't an absolute; it was the story I was believing and acting upon. I could tell myself the same story about living my passion. I could rationalize that my security was better placed in my ability to work hard and to create a successful life.

If you're in a good job, with a good life and a comfortable existence but you want more, I'm talking to you. Our lives aren't meant to be spent adding dollars to our bank accounts or in the case of an employee, adding dollars to your bosses' and the company's bank accounts. We are meant to bring value to the world around our passions. We are each uniquely suited to deliver many things to the world. Is your job cheating you of the time or ability to live out your dream? Are you doing the work that you could be the best in the world at?[1]

When did our lives become just about work? Take a second right now and think about all of the big decisions you have made in your life. Did many surround or have some component of work involved? Where you live? How much you make? Your daily schedule? Your vacation times?

How much of your life is influenced by your job?

I'm not saying everyone needs to leave their job and become an entrepreneur right now. That's not the point. The point is to look at your priorities and consider where along those lines you are putting your passion and mission in life. One of the things I want to help people do with this book is to realize that you have a purpose and were created for a reason. If your job isn't that reason, all I'm saying is you need to figure out how you can spend more time in your purpose.

We all know what will help to make us feel more fulfilled. We all know what we want to be able to do more of in our lives. For me, it was total time control. I wanted to run my schedule; I wanted the clinic to work without me being there. I wanted freedom. I was sacrificing too much of my time working.[2] As a result, too many things were being shuffled around this work schedule.

Because of this work "security," I was willing to shuffle almost every other aspect of my life around in order to keep it. I realized my priorities were off, and I needed a change. At that point, I had only written one book and had put on a few live events. I was in the beginning phases of creating my personal-development company, but I knew it was time to go all in.

Did I just up and leave medicine? No. I significantly cut my work hours. I went from working seven days a week to gradually working less and less. This allowed me time to do more and more of what I was passionate about.[3]

Practicing medicine at one point in my life was all I wanted to do, but that's the beauty of the journey I mentioned in the introduction. Your destiny is filled with many different assignments, but when you feel the tugging on your heart to move on, it's time.

The security you may think your job is providing in your life is just a facade. It is just something you have convinced yourself of, and this can work in the opposite way. You can convince yourself that betting on you is more secure than betting that your employer will keep you no matter what. I say double down on you, and use your life the way it was intended to be used. Your gifts and talents are meant to be shared with the world. Since we spend the majority of our time at work, it is only logical that your work should include your passions.

Surroundings

Being comfortable can also be influenced by your surroundings. If you are in a place where you are at the top or one of the most successful people you know, this can be working to hold you back from dreaming bigger and taking more risks. In this position, it is very easy to draw your identity from your position and surroundings and make it about you.[4] Your position in your surroundings somehow becomes a part of who you are. Even though this is all external, we tend to want to make it an intricate part of who we are. We are not our job titles; we are not our address; we are not what we drive.

There have been many seemingly successful people who have lost it all and then taken their lives. Why do you think someone would commit suicide after losing a job or a title or any sum of money? Because they made those things bigger than what they really were. They convinced themselves that was most of who they were. The balance was tipped into valuing the things more than they valued their own lives. I want us all to understand that the value lies in you. *You* are the masterpiece; you are to be protected and valued. All other things can pass away.[5]

Going back to being comfortable, you can draw a sense of comfort from being at the top. When you're the person everyone looks to for help, it's seductive. You like the role; you love the status and work to keep it all the same. The question is, can you outgrow your surroundings? Can you do greater things? Can you provide more of an impact?

I've been told and have read numerous times in my life that if you're the smartest or richest person in the room, you're in the wrong room. Why is this advice so common? Because it is always very important to keep inspiration in your sights. You have to know where you're going.

The opposite can also be true. If you are surrounded by things that don't inspire you, this can work to dim your light. These types of surroundings can push your dreams down, make them seem impossible or unworthy. If you constantly look around and see things that are dim and dull, where can you find inspiration to live your vision if no one else around you is living theirs?

This unfortunately traps many people into staying in the same place their entire lives. It can make people think this is all there is to life, that their vision isn't realistic. Many describe this as a generational curse, something that is passed from generation to generation unconsciously.

When I was growing up, my family didn't have a lot of money. We had a lot of love, but money always seemed to be lacking. I never lived in a fancy neighborhood, and I never went to private school. There were times when we lost services like electricity or water at our home because of nonpayment.

Many of the conversations I heard growing up were about money—how to get more of it and how to work harder. The visions people described weren't about living their dreams; in many cases, they were about paying their bills or having some cash in their pocket. Some talked about things like lending people money or getting their money back from someone.

The visions I heard talked about around me were at their best to live comfortably, maybe have enough money to pay rent or get a nice car. It was never about net worth or being wealthy or owning things or creating companies.[6] This isn't all of what life is about, but I'm using this example to illustrate that your conversations and visions can be influenced by your surroundings.

Here's the key with surroundings: you must be intentional with reminding yourself what is truly possible. If you can't physically go there, pick up a book and read about it. Dream about it. Visualize about it. Many of the things we have told ourselves about how hard something will be or how long it will take are all lies. We can disprove them with just a little bit of research.

See the World and Dream Big

Traveling (and the accompanying experiences) is the best way to help you with visualization. When you leave your comfortable surroundings and see what else is in the world, you tend to broaden your view. I remember when I was in ground school (flight training) in the air force. We were learning to fly and were on our nighttime-instrument portion of the curriculum. We were to do an out-and-back, which basically means we were to fly somewhere, land, and then come back. We were going to dinner in another city and then going to fly back. Up to that point, I had never just flown somewhere simply to have dinner and then turned around and come back.

This experience opened my mind up to what was truly possible with aviation. I could fly somewhere to my favorite restaurant (within a reasonable distance, obviously) and fly back home the same night! It blew my mind, but it was the experience that was the catalyst that got me thinking.

Seek out experiences that stretch your imagination; try new things; go new places. You never know what specific aspect of the experience will inspire you. Traveling is one of my favorite things to do for this very reason. When you shake up your routine and get outside of the box, I've learned, inspiration comes.

The question becomes, are your surroundings lifting you up or keeping you comfortable? If you're living a comfortable life and stay in your comfort zone most days, it's probably holding you back. Now you are aware of this interesting aspect of comfort, and it's time to do something about it.

I wanted to include this chapter on comfort because this isn't typically what people will point to as what is holding them back. You usually don't hear, "Well, the reason I'm not living a passionate life is because I'm just so darn comfortable!" Most people settle into an existence that doesn't rock the boat, but it's in the rocking that the fun happens!

Family Ties

A subset of your surroundings includes your family. Depending on where you are from, the mind-sets of your family can be implanted in you. If these various mind-sets aren't healthy, they can seriously hinder your progress toward living out your vision. I mention family specifically because you'll always have them around and in your life, so it's in your best interest to identify when your family is holding you back and limit its effect.

Family is a great source of inspiration for many, myself included. In fact, my family is the reason I work so hard. They are the reason I decided to live my dream. I want to be a great example for my children. My wife is my biggest supporter. There are certain people in my family who work to drain energy. They may always have a crisis going on; there may always be drama in their lives, or they may be in a bind or need something.

The idea here is to surround yourself with uplifting people the majority of the time. Said another way, limit your time with people who drain your energy, even if it's family! I know that can be difficult to hear.

Your mind-set and motivation are valuable. If you intend to do something great, you must protect this at all times.[7] Many people have heard the belief that you are the sum of the five people you spend most of your time with. If you are trying to advance in a specific area of your life, find a mentor who is where you want to be, and spend as much time with him or her as possible.

Finally, in this chapter on comfort, I want to talk about pride. You may be asking yourself, what does pride have to do with being comfortable? I'd say everything! Let me explain.

Is Pride Holding You Back?

Pride keeps you in your comfort zone.

Pride, in its purest form, can be a healthy thing. There is nothing wrong with being proud of an accomplishment or the accomplishments of those close to you, but pride can also keep you trapped if you aren't careful.

When you have too much pride, you may think you are above certain things in life. I've found this can be healthy if you are setting standards for your life. It is great to have high standards and work hard to bring them about. I'm not talking about shooting for the stars. How can pride keep you stuck?

As I work with people who are trying to create a vision for themselves, we sometimes run into roadblocks concerning things a person is unwilling to do. I'll start with some basic things. Say I'm working with a new author no one knows. I may say, "Hey, would you be willing to sell your book out of the trunk of your car? Or would you be willing to just talk to people on the street concerning your book?" Some may say, "I'm not going to do that! I'm not going to hustle my book on the streets."

Wait—isn't your book worth selling? Isn't it great content? Well, why wouldn't you want to tell people about it?

Before you say, "Well, that's not my strength; going up to talk to people," this was just one example of a person unwilling to do things that could potentially help progress toward a vision. I could go on and on with examples of things people are unwilling to do to move toward their goal. I'm not talking about unethical things; I'm talking wholesome hard work people just aren't willing to do.

The basis for their denial is centered in pride, the thought that a task is beneath them. I remember when I first started speaking. I would go to high schools and ask for a meeting with the principal. On several occasions, I was turned away. I could have had the thought that these schools should have been glad I was offering to spend time with their students, but this would have come from pride and pride alone.

Stay Humble

Staying humble, even during success, is key to your ability to continue to grow and move forward. We must, no matter how successful, stay open to doing the work, grinding or hustling. It's all the same thing in the end. The idea is not to wait and let failure bring you to humility but to stay humble along the way.

The reality is, none of us is above any task; we all must start from somewhere. That willingness to start at the bottom with a vision to move forward is critical. Don't let the fact that something seems "beneath you" keep you from taking steps that could eventually help you. Stay open to the work, the process, and keep the mind of a servant and student. These will serve you well throughout your journey of pursuing your dream and vision. See it, feel it, and trust it.[8]

Beat: *I'm comfortable*

Start: Getting outside of your comfort zone

Conclusion

Making Your Story

Now that we've covered the top ten excuses that are standing in your way and how to beat them and live the life of your dreams, it's time to start creating your story. Up to this point, you have been preparing for your mission. The lessons you have learned, the experiences you have had, all are of use to you in this moment. There isn't a mistake that has happened; all has been with meaning and has happened *for* you. Let's make the story yours now!

Gone are the days of listening to fear or self-doubt; now it is time to take action. Understanding that you have the power to influence every aspect of your life is the beginning of creating the life you want for yourself. Remember, this isn't going to be easy. When any of the excuses covered in this book come into your mind, revisit the chapter and get a better perspective.

A big inspiration for this book was the late Dr. Wayne Dyer.[1] I love the work he did on excuses and would recommend you read any book of his. Since you made it this far, I know you're serious about getting what you want out of life. Quitting isn't the way to success, and you have dedicated yourself to becoming more resilient. I congratulate you on making it through the book and attacking all the excuses in your life. I am very proud of you.

Living your life and creating it are two totally different mind-sets. Right now, I want you to move toward a mind-set that you are dedicated to creating the life that you want and not just living it. As a part of that, I would encourage you to have a life plan—that means a five-year, ten-year, and twenty-year vision.[2] Knowing where you want to go is one of the biggest hurdles. I would image if you're reading a book on persistence, you probably have a good idea of some of the things you want to accomplish in life. Now it's about making that story.

Imagine you are the director of a movie about your life. What would be the main themes of the movie? What would be the takeaway message? Right now, you are writing the script. You're not done yet. The plot continues to evolve, but how are you planning for the story to end?

When we think about life from a scripted standpoint, we can see how we are the director. We can script it as we may. There isn't one good movie that doesn't involve struggle. So the struggle, however intense it may be, is part of it all. Many of us probably aren't willing to write the struggles in, but there will always be things to overcome. Your hope in the future determines your reaction. Stay hopeful, see the blessing in struggle, and write an amazing story!

What does living your dreams look like to you? Where can you begin? As we discussed in chapter 6, the right time is now. There is no room to wait any longer; it's time.

Taking the First Steps

What will you do? How will you start to move in the direction of your dreams? I would first start by setting goals with timelines. If there isn't a date attached to a wish, it's just that, a wish. When you put a date on it, it's now a goal. Start with some goals and a timeline.

Is it time freedom you are seeking? Is it more income? Is it more happiness? Is it fulfillment? Love?

Now is the time to commit to the first steps. In order to take control of your life, you must decide in this moment that things will change. We've thrown out all of your excuses as to why things aren't possible. We've built the case against quitting, and the defense will now rest. You can do this; you've got what it takes. Let's get to acting like it.

First steps are always scary, but stay focused on greatness. Ignore the distraction that says *focus on fear*. When we are moving toward our dreams, we are able to build and create momentum. This momentum is based in action. Throwing fear to the side, we are able to stick our necks out and claim the vision we have for our lives.

Don't let today end without taking some steps in this moment to start the momentum. This can be a very small step, like making a call list for tomorrow or writing that book title on a piece of paper. It doesn't matter what you do; it only matters that you take action.

Taking action is powerful. It teaches the brain that we are serious about this goal. When we move (take action), we solidify the journey into our brains. We show ourselves this isn't just another thought; this is something we are committed to bringing to pass.

Here's the thing with momentum: you must keep moving every day. Every single day, you must take a step toward your vision. Keep taking steps—baby steps, big steps, small steps. All motion toward your vision counts. This is where most people lose the battle—they don't commit to daily action.

Some days might be easier than others, but you must tap into your discipline in order to deliver day in and day out. Go back to why you're doing this in the first place. Revisit chapter 9 on motivation, for tips on how to get yourself to move when you don't feel like it.

If you're looking to get a launch into your momentum, I would recommend attending one of my live Impact, Purpose, & Destiny Seminars. I do at least one a year in various cities across the United States and abroad. For more info, visit www.ipdseminars.com and sign up for updates.

Enjoy the Ride

Before we get too entrenched with discipline and regimen, I want to remind everyone that this has to be fun! Living your dreams creates the ultimate vision for your life and should be exciting every day. Just think about how great it's going to be, and then transform that into the now.

You have access to those feelings right now. There is no reason you have to wait to feel a certain way when you're working on your dreams every day. You don't have to wait for everything to be perfect before you give yourself the gift of feeling great.

We discussed expectations in chapter 9, when you expect your vision to come to pass and you're dedicated to the work. It's just a matter of time. Celebrate now for the success of the future. Celebrate now for the decision to do it. Celebrate now for the commitment to bring your life into the vision you would like it. Celebrate living the dream now!

There will be valleys, but this is a part of the journey. There will be the unexpected, but this is where your faith and belief kick in. You must believe God has positioned the world to work for you, not against you. God gave you the gifts you are using, and He is working in your favor, even during the tough times when you can't see it.

The beauty of it all is that even during the trials, you are building courage and confidence. Even during the desperation, your vision stays high, and you keep your eyes on the horizon. Don't stall to look down at the obstacles; you're moving toward your destiny. You are always right where you're supposed to be. There aren't any missteps, and the ones who have weathered the storm once are less shaken when the storms come again.

Dig deep when it gets tough! I believe in you. You have what it takes.

Serve the world with your gifts. Here's to persisting in *service*.

God bless and Godspeed.

Appendix

A Reader's Guide to Exercising Persistence

Chapter Exercises

Chapter 1 - Fear

1. Beat Fear of Rejection
   A. Resolve to consider the positive alternative just as intently as the negative.
   B. Only hold the thought of what you want to happen in your mind.
   C. Take five minutes and visualize yourself celebrating.
2. Beat Fear of Failure
   A. Write out completely what your ultimate fear would look like.
   B. List out your best guess at the odds of every item listed happening.
3. Beat Fear of Embarrassment
   A. Make your vision big enough to be worth the risk.
   B. Create your fear curriculum.
      i. Example: Dance in line or sing in public.
4. Beat Fear by Changing Our Beliefs
   A. Ask yourself, *what do I truly believe?*

        i. My dream is most likely possible.
        ii. My dream is a long shot.
    B. Direct your mind toward your vision and choose to believe it is possible.
    C. Act in your new belief.
 5. Beat Fear by Observing Our Thoughts
    A. When you notice yourself thinking a fearful thought, change it to a powerful thought.
    B. Think about how you have power to change things.
    C. Track the amount of time you spend considering how you can make your dream a reality, versus thinking of how things won't work.
 6. Beat Fear by Taking Action
    A. Create a massive action list.
    B. Move in the face of challenge and fear.
        i. Use fear as a guide for your next move.

Chapter 2 - Self-Doubt

 1. Beat Self-Doubt with Worthiness
    A. List to yourself what you are worth, not in financial terms, but in terms of life experience.
    B. Answer the question "Am I worthy of living my dream?"
    C. If your answers to these questions aren't empowering, change your position and allow yourself to begin to think of yourself as worthy.
    D. Look yourself in the mirror daily and say, "I am worthy."
 2. Beat Self-Doubt without Comparisons
    A. Remove all comparisons from your mind by devaluing them.
    B. Use the fair comparison rule if you must compare. Compare yourself with people who have more *and* people who have less.
    C. Beware of the imposter syndrome, and replace those thoughts by reinforcing your prior successes.

    D. See naysayers for what they are, and remove their discouragement from your inner dialogue.
3. Beat Self-Doubt with Confidence
    A. Prepare a preparation guide for everything you need to improve in.
    B. Set the bar higher for practice than is needed for the game.
    C. Place trust in your preparation practices, not innate skill.

Chapter 3 - Money

1. Focus on Value Instead of Money Needed
    A. Bringing value—assess how you are bringing value to the marketplace in your current role.
    B. Creating value—list ways that you can take your current skills and add value in the world. This value add cannot require money.
    C. Communicating value—list the problems you are solving; identify ways you are different than your competition.
2. Be Creative
    A. Crowdsource your funds by identifying investors who understand your value proposition.
    B. Teach yourself to do the little things to cut down on cost initially.
    C. Bring on family members as part of your team.
    D. Sell your product before manufacturing is complete.
3. Start Small
    A. Break down big goals into digestible chunks.
    B. Be willing to take a second job to save money.
    C. Cut costs to streamline your income.

Chapter 4 - Time

1. Seventy-Two-Hour Time Journal
    A. Track your time in fifteen-minute intervals for the next seventy-two hours. How are you really spending your time?

    B. Compare time spent on your dream versus time spent on the dreams of others.
2. Finding Your Why
    A. Ask yourself why you are doing what you do. Ask why again at least five more times.
    B. Sign up for the Purpose-Focused Formula Course. Use discount code: PERSIST.
3. Crystallize Your Vision
    A. Write down your greatest vision for your life in as much detail as possible.
    B. When you do you want to be there? What is standing in your way?
    C. What can you do today to help you get closer to your vision?
4. Identify Your Number-One Priority in Life
    A. Begin to include this priority in every decision in your life.
5. Finding Time
    A. Carve out one hour a day to dedicate to building your dream.
    B. Schedule everything else around this one hour.
    C. Identify down time during your day that you could use if you were intentional.
        i. Instead of listening to music in the car, listen to podcasts or audiobooks in order to continue to learn and improve.
6. Turn Shoulds into Musts
    A. Brainstorm about all the shoulds you have in life, and work to make each one a must during the next few weeks of your life.
7. Schedule Social-Media Time
    A. From your seventy-two-hour journal, identity how much time you are on social-media sites.
    B. Place time in your schedule to connect with friends and family and *only* do social media during those times.

Chapter 5 - Know-How

1. Beat "Lucky" Thinking
   A. Start taking the actions you think will increase your luck.
   B. Ask people you admire about what it took to gain their success.
   C. Research conferences, associations, and networking opportunities in your passion to increase the odds that you will meet someone who can help you.
   D. Every time you think someone is lucky, commit to learning that person's story.
2. Stop Making Realistic Goals
   A. Ask yourself if you are limiting any aspect of your dream and why.
   B. Let go of all realistic thinking, and rewrite your goals without limits.
3. Google "How to [Insert Your Dream Here]
   A. Identify ten steps you can take to move you closer to your goal.
   B. Place those steps into your calendar for accomplishment in the next ten weeks.
4. Talk It Up
   A. Ask ten people a day about their vision, and tell them about yours as well.
   B. Follow up on every lead that is given to you concerning your dream.
5. Find a Mentor
   A. Research people who are where you want to be.
      i. Reach out to them and ask for a chance to interview them about their story.
      ii. After the interview, ask if they are open to mentoring you.
6. Study Your Field
   A. Learn as much as you can about the industry you are interested in.

B. Seek out conferences, interviews, seminars, and podcasts that are related.
7. Start the "Next-Step-Only" Strategy
   A. Take action toward your vision, and only think about the next step.

Chapter 6 - Timing

1. Ask Yourself When Is the Perfect Time for Your Vision to Happen
   A. What is required? How much money or free time will you need?
   B. What else?
2. Consider Starting Right Now—What Is the Worst Thing that Could Happen?
   A. Go back to exercise 2 from chapter 1. List out the worst-case scenario.
   B. Ask yourself, "Why not me, why not now?"
3. Too Young
   A. What are some advantages of being young?
   B. Do you think some older people would like more of these traits?
4. Too Old
   A. What are some advantages of having experience?
   B. Is there value in sharing any of these advantages?
5. It's Already Been Done
   A. List some people who have done what you want to do.
   B. What can you learn from them blazing the trail for you?
      i. How can you better your efforts with this information?
6. Timing and the Marketplace for Entrepreneurs
   A. Differentiation—what is different about what you are offering?
      i. What is the best way to communicate this to your potential customer?
      ii. How do you plan on competing in the market?

      B. Value—what additional value can you bring to the market?
      C. Remember, it isn't always an A-or-B question for customers.
          i. You can be an A-and-B product addition.

Chapte 7 - Circumstances

1. What Circumstances Have You Told Yourself Are Holding You Back?
   A. How can you change your mind-set around this issue?
      i. Can you use this to consider it an advantage?
2. Read Viktor Frankl's *A Man's Search for Meaning*
   A. In what areas in your life do you need to work on your attitude?
3. What Adversity Have You Been Through in Life that Has Grown You?
   A. What current adversity could you see as a learning experience?
      i. What lesson are you learning?
4. In What Areas in Life Have You Compromised?
   A. Have these compromises cost you your dream?
   B. What would it mean to you and your family if you started living your dream now?
5. Remove the Phrase, "I Had No Choice" from Your Language
   A. What empowering phrase could you replace this with?

Chapter 8 - Failure

1. Objectify Failure
   A. Was it your strategy that failed or your efforts?
   B. Is it possible to get a different result if you change your approach?
2. Commit to Preparation
   A. After failure, focus on a different preparation strategy for the next try.

B. Analyze how you prepared initially, and ask what you can do differently.
   C. Your "best" can be improved upon
3. Look for the Lesson in Failure
   A. Ask, "What can I learn from this failure?"
   B. Focus on how you can improve from this failure.
4. Growth through Failure
   A. Pushing through failure builds your tolerance for persisting.
   B. Look at failure as tolerance development.
5. Who Could Benefit from Hearing Your Failure Story?
   A. Focus on impact instead of impressing others.
   B. Find someone who is struggling with something you once struggled with, and commit to helping them crush it!
6. Harness the Power of Desperation
   A. Harness that desperation energy.
   B. Channel it into your next effort.

Chapter 9 - Motivation

1. Periodic Reflection on *Why*
   A. Why is this important to you? To whom does this matter?
   B. Weekly go over your reason for wanting your goal, and reflect on what it is about.
2. Connect Your Busyness to Your Overall Goal or Purpose
   A. How is what I'm doing right now connect to my goal?
3. Journal Daily
   A. Discuss your struggles and successes in your journal every day.
      i. Review in times of struggle or when you want to quit.
   B. Celebrate often how far you've come!
4. Cultivate Discipline
   A. Start with consistency.
      i. Track your consistency when it comes to goal-oriented actions.
   B. Focus on the end result of what you are trying to get.

        i. Do so especially in moments of not wanting to take action.
5. Examine Your Belief Systems
   A. Do you believe success is about person or about strategy?
   B. Focus on strategies you can duplicate.
6. What Do You Truly Expect?
   A. Do you really expect to get what you are going after?
   B. Do you believe your efforts will get you there?
7. Focus on Strengths
   A. Make your weaknesses into strengths.
   B. What would you say your weaknesses are?
   C. What are your strengths?
   D. Can either of these be expanded upon? Can you grow in these areas with focused effort?
8. Service Is Everything
   A. Who are you serving on a daily basis with your efforts?
   B. Who else does your mission matter to?
   C. How are you using your life to enhance the lives of others?

Chapter 10 - Comfort

1. Beat Comfort
   A. Do you have a comfortable life with a comfortable salary and a comfortable neighborhood?
   B. Why is comfort the goal?
2. Are You at the Top of Your Circle?
   A. Who in your inner circle is helping to drive you?
   B. Are you comfortable being the one everyone around you looks up to?
3. Do You Believe You Can Do More?
   A. What is stopping you?
4. Does Your Job Run Your Life?
   A. Does every major life decision revolve around your work schedule?
   B. Do you derive most of your self-worth from your position at work?

C. If you wanted to take a vacation right now, whom would you have to ask?
   D. Do you think your job makes your life more secure?
5. Surroundings
   A. What inspires you about your surroundings?
   B. Do you travel regularly to new places?
6. Let Go of Pride
   A. Is there anything your pride is keeping you from doing that could help your vision?
   B. Stay humble, no matter how much success you have.

Acknowledgments

There are many, many people to thank for supporting me in this project. I am forever grateful to my wife, Chenelle Lee, for supporting my time at my desk and keeping the little guys occupied while Daddy works. Thank you to my children, Chanel, Marc, and Caleb Lee, for being my daily motivation to be my best and to lead the way in living my dream.

I am indebted to my immediate family for listening to hours upon hours of me talking about my vision and supporting my dream: to my oldest sister, Monique Lee, for being a sounding board for ideas any time of the day; to my younger sisters, SeQuia Bowie and Symone Williams, I've always strived to make you two proud I was your brother. The same is true for my parents—your support and enthusiasm with every project have driven me to continue to create.

To the home team, the Memphis elite, Hart Robinson and Daniel Watson, I've known you guys almost two decades, and good people are always good people. Thank you for not forgetting me when I moved away!

I'm forever grateful for the support I've received from my medical colleagues Dr. Loretta Williams and Dr. Antonio Webb for their endless support and commitment to helping me make this book a success.

Thank you to my Texas support system, Clarence Williams, Bo Carrington, Anthony Hylick, Ernesto Benavides, and Armando Trevino. Your feedback was priceless!

Similarly, I'm thankful to all of my local support here in California: Caliph Assagai, John Jackson, Otis Amey, Everett Glenn, Marcellene Watson-Derbigny, Michael Harper, Torence Powell, and Eric Gravenberg, who graciously agreed to take a look at the book.

To my BMX family: Jason Richardson, Tony Hoffman, Craig Reynolds, Gregg Frederick, Bryce Betts, and my British brother, Michael Pusey, for treating me and my work as your own from the beginning.

I'd lastly like to acknowledge all of the readers of this text. It is you I had in mind as I created this. Thank you for your support and your continuous spreading of this book's message going forward.

God bless and Godspeed.

—April 2017

Notes

Chapter 1

1 Robert M. Sapolsky, *Why Zebras Don't Get Ulcers: An Updated Guide To Stress, Stress Related Diseases, and Coping.* 2nd Rev Ed (New York, NY: W. H. Freeman, 1998).
2 Seth Godin, *Tribes* (New York, NY: Penguin Group, 2008).
3 Tim Ferriss, *The 4-Hour Work Week* (New York, NY: Crown Publishers, 2009).
4 Napoleon Hill, *Think and Grow Rich* (Chatsworth, CA: Wilshire Book Company, 1999).
5 Abbott, M.J., Rapee, R.M. 'Post-event rumination and negative self-appraisal in social phobia before and after treatment.' *Journal of Abnormal Psychology.* (2004): 136-144
6 Grant Cardone, *The 10X Rule* (Hoboken, NJ: John Wiley & Sons, Inc., 2011).
7 Anthony Robbins, *Awaken the Giant Within* (New York, NY: Free Press, 1991).

Chapter 2

1 Jack Canfield, *The Success Principles* (New York, NY: HarperCollins Publishers, 2005).
2 Henry Cloud, *The Law of Happiness* (New York, NY: Howard Books, 2011).
3 Brendon Burchard, *The Millionaire Messenger* (New York, NY: Morgan James Publishing, 2011).
4 Sakulku, J., Alexander, J. 'The Imposter Phenomenon.' *International Journal of Behavioral Science.* 6 (2011): 73-92
5 Sheldon, Kennon M. and Laura King. 'Why Positive Psychology is Necessary.' *American Psychologist* 56 (2001): 216-217

6 Napoleon Hill, *Think and Grow Rich* (Chatsworth, CA: Wilshire Book Company, 1999).
7 Jason Richardson, *It's All BS! We're All Wrong and You're All Right* (San Jose, CA: Substantium, Inc., 2015)
8 Karl E. Weick, 'Small Wins: Redefining the Scale of Social Problems," *American Psychologist* 39 (1984): 40-49

Chapter 3

1 Michael Gerber, *The E Myth Revisited* (New York, NY: HarperCollins Publishers, 1995).
2 Dale Carnegie, *How to Win Friends & Influence People* (New York, NY: Pocket Books, 1936).
3 Walter Isaacson, *Steve Jobs* (New York, NY: Simon & Schuster, 2011)
4 Mark Cuban, *How to Win at the Sport of Business* (New York, NY: Diversion Books, 2011).
5 Dave Ramsey, *Financial Peace Revisited* (New York, NY: Viking Penguin, 2003).
6 Thomas J Stanley, *Stop Acting Rich... And Start Living Like a Real Millionaire.* (Hoboken, NJ: John Wiley & Sons, Inc., 2009).

Chapter 4

1 Sharon Salzberg, *Real Happiness at Work* (New York, NY: Workman Publishing, 2014).
2 Spencer Johnson, *Who Moved My Cheese?* (New York, NY: G.P. Putnam's Sons, 2002).
3 Stephen Covey, *The 7 Habits of Highly Effective People* (New York, NY: Free Press, 2004).
4 Greg McKeown, *Essentialism* (New York, NY: Crown Business, 2014).
5 David Allen, *Getting Things Done* (New York, NY: Penguin Books, 2015).
6 Malcolm Gladwell, *Tipping Point* (New York, NY: Back Bay: 2002).
7 Blair S N, Kohl H W, 3rd, Paffenbarger R S., Jr et al. "Physical fitness and all cause mortality. A prospective study of healthy men and women." *JAMA*. 1989 Nov 3;262(17):2395-401

Chapter 5

1 Malcolm Gladwell, *Outliers* (New York, NY: Little, Brown and Company, 2008).
2 Russell Simmons, *Do You!* (New York, NY: Gotham Books, 2007).

3   Manny Khoshbin, *Contrarian Playbook* (Los Gatos, CA: Smashwords, 2012).
4   Jack Canfield, *The Success Principles* (New York, NY: HarperCollins Publishers, 2005).
5   Seth Godin, *Tribes* (New York, NY: Penguin Group, 2008).
6   Paulo Coelho, *The Alchemist* (New York, NY: HarperCollins Publishers, 2006).
7   Charles Duhigg, *The Power of Habit* (New York, NY: Random House, 2014).
8   Ryan Blair, *Nothing to Lose, Everything to Gain* (New York, NY: Penguin Group, 2010).

Chapter 6

1   Joel Osteen, *Your Best Life Now* (New York, NY: Warner Faith, 2004).
2   Robin Sharma, *The Monk Who Sold His Ferrari* (New York, NY: HarperCollins Publishers, 1997).
3   Michael Hyatt, *Platform* (Nashville, TN: Thomas Nelson, 2012).
4   Jason Richardson, *It's All BS! We're All Wrong and You're All Right* (San Jose, CA: Substantium, Inc., 2015)
5   Malcolm Gladwell, *Outliers* (New York, NY: Little, Brown and Company, 2008).

Chapter 7

1   Viktor Frankl, *A Man's Search for Meaning* (Boston, MA: Beacon Press, 1959).
2   A. L. Duckworth et al., "Grit: Perseverance and Passion for Long-Term Goals," *Journal of Personality and Social Psychology* 92 (2007).
3   "Dyslexic entrepreneurs-why they have a competitive edge" *The Guardian*, 2015, accessed March 28, 2017, http://www.theguardian.com/small-business-network/2015/jan/15/dyslexic-entrepreneurs-competitive-edge-business-leaders
4   Malcolm Gladwell, *David and Goliath* (New York, NY: Little, Brown and Company, 2013).
5   Clarence M. Lee, Jr., *Well, My Mom Says...* (Bloomington, IN: WestBow Press, 2014).
6   Rick Warren, *The Purpose-Driven Life* (Grand Rapids, MI: Zondervan, 2002).
7   Carol S. Dweck, *Mindset* (New York, NY: Random House, 2006).

Chapter 8

1. Eckhart Tolle, *The Power of Now* (Novato, CA: New World Library, 1997).
2. Alan Morinis, *Everyday Holiness* (Boston, MA: Trumpeter Books, 2007).
3. Sheina Orbell et al., "Motivational and Volitional Processes in Action Initiation: A Field Study of the Role of Implementation Intentions," *Journal of Applied Social Psychology* 30, no. 4 (April 2000).
4. Tim Harford, *Adapt: Why Success Always Starts with Failure* (New York, NY: Picador, 2011).
5. A. L. Duckworth et al., "Self-Discipline Outdoes IQ in Predicting Academic Performance of Adolescents," *Psychological Science* 16 (2005).
6. Roy F Baumeister et al., "Self-Regulation and Depletion of Limited Resources: Does Self-Control Resemble a Muscle?" *Psychological Bulletin* 126 (2000).
7. Angela Duckworth, *Grit: The Power of Passion and Perseverance* (New York, NY: Scribner, 2016).

Chapter 9

1. Walter Isaacson, *Steve Jobs* (New York, NY: Simon & Schuster, 2011)
2. T. D. Jakes, *Destiny* (New York, NY: FaithWords, 2015).
3. Stephen Covey, *The 7 Habits of Highly Effective People* (New York, NY: Free Press, 2004).
4. J.P. Tangney et al., "High-Self Control Predicts Good Adjustment, Less Pathology, Better Grades, and Interpersonal Success," Journal of Personality 72, no. 2 (2004).
5. Lawrence M. Hanser et al., *United States Service Academy Admissions: Selecting for Sucess at the Military Academy/West Point and as an Officer* (Santa Monica, CA: RAND Corporation, 2015).
6. Anders Ericsson, *Peak: Secrets From the New Science of Expertise* (Houghton Mifflin Harcourt Publishing Company, 2016).

Chapter 10

1. Jim Collins, *Good to Great* (New York, NY: HarperBusiness, 2001).
2. D. Fassel, *Working ourselves to death: The high cost of workaholism, the rewards of recovery.* (San Francisco, CA: Harper Collins, 1990).
3. Dave Ramsey, *EntreLeadership* (New York, NY: Howard Books, 2011).
4. Max Lucado, *It's Not About Me* (Brentwood, TN: Integrity, 2004).
5. Bruce Piasecki, *Doing More With Less* (Hoboken, NJ: John Wiley & Sons, 2012).

6   T. Harv Eker, *Secrets of the Millionaire Mind* (New York, NY: HarperBusiness, 2005).
7   Norman V Peale, *The Power of Positive Thinking* (New York, NY: Fireside, 1952.
8   David Cook, *Golf's Sacred Journey* (Grand Rapids, MI: Zondervan, 2006).

Conclusion

1   Wayne Dyer, Excuses Begone (Carlsbad, CA: Hay House, 2009).
2   Michael Hyatt and Daniel Harkavy, *Living Forward* (Grand Rapids, MI: Baker Books, 2016).

Author Bio

Clarence Lee Jr. is a nationally celebrated author, international speaker, and CEO of CMLEEJR Co., LLC, a personal-development brand that conducts seminars on high performance and mental conditioning for teams, organizations, and students.

Dr. Lee holds a degree in biology from the University of the Incarnate Word and degrees in medicine (MD) and business (MBA) from Drexel University. A decorated war veteran, he served in the United States Air Force as a flight surgeon, flying the T-38 and U-2 airframes. He was recently named Top 40 Under 40 by the *Sacramento Business Journal* (2014) and Drexel University (2016). He has been featured in several media outlets, including ABC, CBS, FOX, *Black Enterprise*, *Essence*, *Live Happy*, and *Becker's Hospital Review*.

Dr. Lee lives in California with his wife and three children. As a Christian, he believes we all have God-given talents and purpose, and it's his mission to assist you in living yours.

Read his latest thoughts on fulfillment, achievement, and lifestyle creation at www.clarenceleejr.com.

Made in the USA
Las Vegas, NV
09 November 2024

11390489R00090